Dedication

To the Lightworkers who are dedicated to following Spirit with each breath and each step; who are dedicated to embodying Divinity and living Heaven on Earth; who are dedicated to joyous service, fierce wholeness, impeccability, and the cosmic joke; and who are dedicated to a vision of planetary ascension that is easy, graceful, ecstatic, and high-velocity fun. Ya-hoo!

WHAT IS LIGHTBODY?
ARCHANGEL ARIEL, CHANNELED BY TACHI-REN

© 1990, 1995 , 1999 by Tashira Tachi-ren
Published 1990. Second Edition 1995. Third Edition 1999.

Third Edition

Published by:

World Tree Press
401 Thornton Road
Lithia Springs, Georgia 30122

Library of Congress Cataloging-in-Publication Data
Ariel (Archangel : Spirit)
What is Lightbody / material channeled from Archangel Ariel by Tachi-ren.

Cover redesigned by sarawonder

ISBN-13 978-0-9627209-5-6 $14.95

Printed in United States of America

What is Lightbody?

Archangel Ariel
Channeled by Tashira Tachi-ren

Published by

WORLDTREE PRESS

Table of Contents

Tashira's Acknowledgments 1994 Edition

Special thanks to:

Suzane Coronis, my beloved, for her constant wisdom, outrageous laughter, and steady reminders to make it fun.

Tony Stubbs, flow director extraordinaire, for working his hoofies to the bone to make this book happen. You were there for me from the beginning. See, I really couldn't have done this one without you. Awesome!

J.J. Wilson, for your incredible insight, humor, fierceness, and love. You keep Angelic Outreach together, body and soul — we couldn't do it without you.

Gary Johnson, creator of the beautiful Alpha Chamber, for his financial and spiritual support of this project. Because of you, we didn't have to just "beat it flat."

Delightful Dolores Montoya, for transcribing the tapes and covering the planet with rainbows and fairy dust.

Paul Bader, for transcribing the additions to the text in the midst of chaos.

Susannah Redelfs, for proofing the text and making each of us laugh, even when it hurt.

Extraterrestrial Earth Mission, for their excellent stimulation and relentless humor. We just love you guys!

Ralph Edmonds, Lucie Geear, Mark Kramer, Arisha and Zeke Wenneson, Lea Hubbard, Faraday Tabler, Michelle La Prise, Barbara Brooks, Arasia, Antarah, and Sue Gage for their financial and Spiritual support of these projects.

Rob Gerard and Cathy Cook of Oughten House, for their vision of getting ascension-oriented materials out on the planet and wanting to include Angelic Outreach in that vision.

Ariel and the Council of Ein Soph (The Crew), for being the best multidimensional support team this embodied angelic Lightworker could ever want.

Sara Benjamin-Rhodes of Celestial Co-operatives, for her excellent editing of *What is Lightbody?* It was wonderful to have an editor who was in alignment with this work. I truly appreciate her precision and forthrightness. I look forward to co-creating with you on a future book.

All the Lightworkers who have loved and supported AO, and have, are, and will use the information in this book to co-create Heaven on Earth. Let's get busy!

Tashira Tachi-ren

Forward to the 1999 Edition

Tashira Tachi-ren walked into the body on July 11, 1985 and walked out of the body on December 17, 1997. With an eternal essence of Divine Will and a divine function of Holographic Harmonization, her divine design was perfectly suited to embody the vision of, and be the primary channel for, the Council of Ein Soph. In July of 1989, Tashira and Suzane Coronis formed *Angelic Outreach* to be the first physical plane expression of the Council's vision of multi-universal ascension. A core group of beings, aligned to the Council's vision, gradually formed.

The Lightbody model described in this book, as well as, the Unified Chakra, are the basis of all other *Angelic Outreach* foundational material. During Tashira's twelve years on planet she brought through a tremendous amount of information, conducted workshops, events, created many audio tape sets, and developed the *Angelic Outreach* Potions. The *Angelic Outreach* products she developed were the beginning of the *Alchemical Mage* catalog. The editing of her archival tape sets continues and these will be available through *Alchemical Mage* in the future.

Our purpose as a group has always been to develop and distribute new tools and technologies for the Council of Ein Soph. All of us experienced tremendous growth working with her techniques. When Tashira walked-out in December 1997, those of us who were the core group of *Angelic Outreach* were faced with the decision of how to best carry on the work she started. Initially, we kept the same name and structure she gifted to us. However, in order to bring in new techniques and tools we needed to expand beyond the original vision and structure of *Angelic Outreach*. *Angelic Outreach,* <u>as an organization,</u> no longer exists.

This model of Lightbody and the Invocations are just as valid and moving as when they were first presented in 1990. In 1995, Ariel revised *What is Lightbody?* for the Oughten House edition. Of course there has been evolution and expansion in the material since then. As the current resident of this body, it fell to me to make the difficult decision whether to include any of the new material in this edition. Much of the new information was channeled through myself and other channels. In consultation with Archangel Ariel, it was decided to allow *What is Lightbody?* to stand virtually as it was published in 1995. The new material is available on tape through *Alchemical Mage*.

This edition features an a Tools section, and full write ups on all of the *Angelic Outreach Potions* brought through by Tashira Tachiren. If you resonate with the material in this book, I encourage you to access the rest of the *Angelic Outreach* foundational material, and perhaps the new potions, elixirs, and information as well.

This is both an exciting and trying time in the planetary ascension process. The mutations are coming more rapidly and consciousness must evolve ever more quickly. Every day brings more opportunities for becoming more awake and in love with Spirit, as well as more opportunities for confusion and limitation. You are completely at choice about what you will make Real in your life. Every decision you make affects the ascension process, as do everyone else's. From my viewpoint, we are here to co-create Heaven on Earth with God itself and with the Godself within all other beings. No greater honor has ever been bestowed upon a species.

Choose to see the pure Soul within all beings,

even though they may not see it within themselves.

Choose to honor the sovereign reality of all beings,

even though their words or actions may hurt you.

Choose to transform through ecstasy and Grace,

even though drama and trauma may seem more natural to you.

Choose to live in this miraculous Now moment,

even though nostalgia, regrets and fear may entice you to not be Present.

Choose to be a blessing to the World and All Life,

even though circumstances may encourage you to harden your heart.

Choose to love others,

even though it may seem naive.

Choose to love God with all your being,

and know that this is all that is really required.

Choose to Live Heaven.

Aliyah Ziondra

Aliyah Merkavah Ziondra walked into the body of Tashira Tachi-Ren on December 17, 1997. As an incarnation of Rapture Elohim, her essence is Divine Rapture and her function is Divine Alignment. She views her orientation as devotional and heart-centered. She specializes in channeling the Elohim verbally, tonally, and energetically and is deeply committed to the Divine co-creative process. Aliyah has created Wings of Glory as the vehicle to express her mystical and inspirational orientation to the Heavenly Merkavah, and to further the on-going work of the Council of Ein Soph. Under the Wings of Glory umbrella are The Shefa Services for her individual alignment sessions, and Rapture Resources for her stories, songs, poetry, and sacred objects. Her elixirs, tapes, and other products are distributed by Alchemical Mage. Through the Merkavah Ein Soph, Kabbalah, and the Keepers of the Legacy of Humanity she works to repair the pathways to God, free the Sparks of Divinity within creation, and assist ecstatic ascension. She delights in assisting people to deepen their connection with Source, experience their relationship to Divinity, and co-create Heaven on Earth. She feels deeply honored to be in embodied service on this beautiful ascending planet.

Preface to the 1995 Edition

On May 30, 1994, a dramatic shift occurred in the Divine Plan for planet Earth. The entire time frame for planetary ascension was accelerated. In the beginning of June, many of you experienced the surfacing of intense survival fear, enemy patterning, and old pictures of reality from your physical bodies. These energies were emerging out of your genetic encodements. It was as if God had reached into your body and was pulling out the fear and separation by the roots. Old physical traumas or illnesses may have briefly reappeared. Time accelerated and many of you feel frustrated about completing projects.

The levels described in the Lightbody model are still valid. Moving through these mutational stages can take many years or a few minutes, depending on the Will of Spirit. *These levels are not a measurement of personal spiritual achievement*. Your Spirit determines your appropriate Lightbody level, depending on your Divine design, your incarnational grid within the hologram, and what is needed to serve the planetary ascension. Truly, Lightbody is about the evolution of this species and the collective service to all life.

If you look at this planet from the viewpoint of your Oversouls, you see its entire Alpha-Omega cycle (from its beginning to its end in time), and zillions of parallel realities across space. You are incarnate parts of the Oversouls and have many lifetimes throughout the space-time fabric, simultaneously. We call this your holographic grid of incarnations. From the viewpoint of the Oversouls, these lives are all happening NOW and are points of coordination for restructuring the hologram of this planetary game of separation. The entire space/time construct is contained in a membrane that we call a holographic bubble. This bubble of third-dimensional realities is currently three-quarters of the way through the fourth dimension and is "rising" rapidly. The bubble is collapsing and dissolving. People are having many different responses to these changes.

A Parable

Imagine that once upon this time, there is a sealed fishbowl (made of one-way glass) inside of a large aquarium. The fish in the aquarium can see into the bowl, but the fish in the bowl cannot see out. Their fishbowl is their only reality. Imagine that the large aquarium is filled with salt water and anemones, crabs, and all kinds of wondrous fishes. The fishbowl is filled with fresh water and goldfish.

The glass of the fishbowl is getting thinner and thinner. Small amounts of salt water are seeping through and the goldfish must evolve very fast to handle this change in their environment. As the wall grows thinner, the goldfish begin to get glimpses of the creatures in the aquarium. Some of the goldfish see these other fishes as The Enemy, and fiercely try to defend their bowl from imminent invasion. They see the anemones as Evil, and accuse other goldfish of being "anemone-influenced." These goldfish hide their personal fear by projecting a climate of fear around them.

Some of the goldfish assume that the fishes in the aquarium have been controlling their fishbowl all along. They see themselves and the other goldfish as hapless victims. They assume that the creatures on the other side of the glass have kept them in the fishbowl just so they could be eaten someday. As their bowl dissolves, they meet each passing day with dread.

Some of the goldfish see the fishes on the other side of the glass as holy, all-powerful superiors. These goldfish relinquish all inner authority and wildly swing from feeling especially chosen to feeling worthless. They try to interpret hidden messages from their "masters" and base their actions and beliefs on the messages. They swim here and there in the bowl, creating lots of ripples, but no lasting effects.

Some of the goldfish see the other creatures as brethren and marvel at the miraculous variations "The Great Fish" has used to express Itself. These goldfish know that the evolution of their species, the dissolving of their bowl, and even the reactions of fear, martyrdom, and unworthiness in the other goldfish are in the fins of "The

Great Fish." They follow the Spirit of The Great Fish with each gill and each fin. They experience ecstasy as they prepare to swim in vaster waters.

So, the holographic bubble is collapsing, at times causing massive parallel mergers numbering in the tens of thousands per minute. Linear time is collapsing as it evolves towards a simultaneous time structure (Infinite NOW). Linear space is expanding, as it evolves towards simultaneous space (Infinite Presence).

Parallel mergers are often disorienting — lots of dizziness, shaking, shimmering vision, and breaches of continuity. Knowing that the parallel mergers in mid-October 1994 would shift people's Lightbody levels and could be so intense that it could collapse the bubble, an experiment was conducted. We stimulated the complex standing waves of the sub-atomic structures to accept standing waves from a higher dimension. This allowed the sub-atomic wave motions in separate parallels to be synchronized into controlled interference patterns. The result was smooth intensification of manifested Light and gentle cancellation of abrasive discontinuities. The holographic bubble was not destabilized; it was actually strengthened.

This means that the final collapse will be much smoother. We will synchronize the complex standing waves of this reality with the standing waves of the high astral plane, and then with those of the higher dimensions. The dimensional transitions will be less of a shock; instead, it will be a more dreamlike experience. We think that everyone will notice the shift, nonetheless.

In mid-October, without much of the usual drama, the majority of Lightworkers moved into tenth-level Lightbody and the overall population moved into eighth-level. Many of you (including Tachi-ren) have complained about the lack of fireworks from this shift. We, too, want people to notice what is happening. Although our primary interest is to not destabilize the bubble prematurely, we will try to increase the intensity of experience from future mergers.

As Spirit is placing you into a new positioning with regard to the ascension, many of you are feeling complete with your work on this plane. Allow old forms and models to gracefully drop away. A new form is evolving. You may find that you are more expressive or that you must be wildly creative. There are two songs out on the airwaves that sum up what most of you are feeling: "All I want to do is have some fun and I think that I'm not the only one," and "Bring it on — don't wait until tomorrow!"

Which fish are you? Are you busy fighting "The Enemy?" Have you pulled out your Light sword and are righteously battling the secret government, the greys, the dark forces, etc.? Does this truly match your vision of Heaven on Earth? Are you focused on extraterrestrials trying to control the Earth? Are you participating with pictures of reality that hold that humankind are victims, dupes, or a colonized food source? How does this mesh with the view that each person is a vast, multidimensional master? Have you exchanged your connection with your own Spirit for one with a guru, an Ascended Master, or a channeled entity? The entire universe will rearrange itself to accommodate your pictures of reality. What do you want — really? Your Spirit is shifting your positioning in relation to ascension. Allow the sweetness of transfiguration to fill your soul. Follow your own beloved Spirit, with each breath and each step. Live Heaven!

Of the Source, in Service to the Source

— The Council of Ein Soph

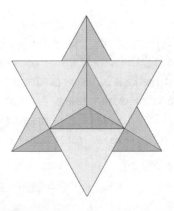

THE CLARION CALL

Parallel merges,
Magnetic surges.
Time collapses,
Straining synapses.
Nothing is wrong —
Bring it on!
Bodies are hurting
From encodements bursting.
Resistance depleted;
Works almost completed.
These changes are strong —
Bring it on!
Physical bodies' communion
Is genetic reunion.
With codes of Infinity
For embodied Divinity.
Our bodies are coming along —
Bring it on!
Mental delusions and
Shattered illusions.
Go through the Gate:
Awakening waits.
Surrender, go on —
Bring it on!
To shift realities
Into Divine Normalities,
It's very effective
To parallax perspective.

For what do you long?
Bring it on!
From transpersonal knowing
Attachments are going.
Emotional upheaval,
Then Spirit is revealed.
The love for the One —
Bring it on!
Open the heart to jubilation,
Open the mind to revelation.
Open the body, open the Soul
To Beloved Spirit's goal.
The mission's nearly done —
Bring it on!
Mystical missions
Need magical visions.
Hearts open and wild
Frees the Magical Child.
We're dancing towards Home —
Bring it on!
Our ecstatic birthright filled
With Grace and de-Light
Is heaven styled
Through the Magical Child.
Touch the new dawn —
Bring it on!
Won't you join in the fun?
Everybody can come
To the Universal Celebration
Of humanity's graduation.

Join in Victory's song —
Bring it on!
Old worlds are ending,
Universes ascending.
Merkabahs' spinning
This world's new beginning.
Call of the One —
Bring it on!
Merkabah merges,
True Love surges.
Space/time collapses,
Spirit enrapts us.
The flight of the One —
Bring it on!

Rapture Elohim
channeled through
Tashira Tachi-ren

Channel's Preface Original Edition

Please take everything you read within these pages as a model and just another opinion. It is impossible to express Truth (with a capital T) in any earthly language. You can only describe realities. I view reality as a verb, not a noun. There is no one great "Reality" with a capital R. It is a constantly shifting co-creation of intersecting individual realities, each absolutely unique. I choose to operate within a reality that planet Earth is ascending into the Light dimensions through Joy and Laughter.

Also, you should know that no channel is one hundred percent accurate. After all, this and all channeled information comes through a filter of human perceptions. So, if something in these pages rings true for you, then it was your Truth all along. If it doesn't, lovingly release it back to the universe. It's just another opinion.

I and my work group ask that you not create me, Ariel, or any channeled entity as an outside authority. You are the only authority over what is "real and true" in your life.

Angelic Outreach (AO) was designed to support incarnate Lightworkers to awaken to their multidimensional vastness, embody Divinity, and to lighten up Planet Earth. In its earthly form, AO created new technologies, techniques, and articulations for the co-creation of Heaven on Earth. With the publication of this book, AO's work is complete. Lightworkers may access AO through tapes, potions, and books like this one.

There are 383 ascending planets, in five local universes, one of which is planet Earth. As a Lightworker, you are probably incarnate on all of them.

Angelic Outreach, at its vastest, is a multidimensional, multi-universal program of full merger with Source. Through all of our incarnations we act like connective tissue between universes, stars, and planets. We help coordinate the various planetary ascension programs within each universe, as well as assist the merger of several universes into one. It acts as the bridge between all of the Creations, joining the Many with the One.

I am a conscious merged channel for Higher Light beings. I expand my consciousness multidimensionally and merge with the vastness of my own Spirit. From there, I merge with my work group of twenty-four Light beings and all of us channel back through my physical body. This is quite an experience, as you can imagine.

My relationship with "The Crew," as I call my work group, is as an equal. We are co-creative Masters, beings of Light, and we see you as Light Masters also.

In this crew, Archangel Ariel usually functions as a Lightbody theoretician. She articulates the Lightbody process, creating models, technologies, and meditations to support the ascension at every level. As one of these embodied aspects of the crew, I function as a channel for the group's energies and as a "hands on" Lightbody technician.

So, the *What is Lightbody?* model presented here is Ariel's "gig," and I think she does it quite well. The material for *What is Lightbody?* was developed and presented in small workshops, from 1987 through 1990. It was transcribed, edited, and printed in book form in 1990. In 1993, the material was updated, revised, and put out on audio cassette. In this Oughten House edition, both Ariel and I have added information throughout the text. We hope you find it a useful and delightful map for the road to Lightbody.

This edition also includes the book *Invocations*. Since its publication in 1989, many Lightworkers have loved these 33 poems, often reading them every day. They were created by various members of "The Crew," and you will feel their different frequencies in the Invocations.

Originally, these two books were self-published by Angelic Outreach and we were never able to keep up with the demand for them. So we are ecstatic that Oughten House will make them available to those of you who have waited so patiently, and to all of you who will read this material for the first time. May your journey into the Light be the path of Joy.

Of the Source, in Service to the Source,

— Tashira Tachi-ren

Introduction by Archangel Ariel

When we look at you, we see you as vast, multidimensional beings. There's just a little bit of you in this body, thinking that you are all of it. Some of you are getting an inkling that's not so. We see you at all dimensions, in the vastness of who you are.

From our viewpoint, because you are reading this, you are a Lightworker and you are here with a job to do. You are here to assist in the transition of planet Earth into Light. You've done it countless times before and you are an expert in your field.

This book presents you with a model which describes what's going on in this process for this planet. It is not truth. It is not real, because when you are attempting to describe a multidimensional, non-linear model, it's impossible to describe it in the English language. But we're going to do our very best. If at times it bounces around, bear with it, because the process itself is not exactly linear. It's a lot more like music.

Now the only way we can present this model is linearly. We have attempted to do it non-linearly and everyone goes brain-dead. We hope that you can feel the shifts you're going through. We know that if your mental body can say, "Ah, this is part of eighth level of Lightbody," it eases the secret fears. There is a need for this information to go out because the fear level is so very high, especially coming from the physical and mental bodies. If you know what's happening to you and know that it's part of a coherent process, then you feel less crazy.

Every time a planet goes to Light, it is a unique expression of returning home from the experience of separation. The process differs, depending on the particular planet and species that's going to Light. This model is for the human species on planet Earth.

There are 383 other planets also going to Light simultaneously, and most of you are incarnate on most of them. This planet is special, however, because it has experienced the maximum separation from the Source and now it is returning. It will be successful. There is absolutely no doubt that this planet's return to the Source will be successful, and there will be no apocalypse in this parallel reality. There was a time when we were not so sure that this planet would be able to go home, but now we are celebrating the certainty of a safe return.

Now, a species can ascend or go to Light without the planet ascending. You are not the first species to ascend from this planet — there have been four other races before you. What makes this particular process so exquisitely wonderful is that planet Earth is ascending also. She is a conscious, living entity who agreed to support this game of separation on the condition that she would ascend at its conclusion.

We'd like to mention the exquisiteness of this game as it returns to the Source. The beauty of your Divine Expression as you return is so wondrous for us to watch. Even though you stepped away from the Source for what is to us only a brief time, your reunification is one of the most exquisite energies in the universe. We look forward to you consciously experiencing this for yourselves. Because we exist in simultaneity, we have already seen you enjoy your reunification, and we look forward to sharing your joy when you catch up with yourselves.

I would also like to mention that the measurement for our model of Lightbody comes from looking at the amount of adenosine triphosphate in the cells. We measure Lightbody levels from your physical body's level of mutation. Now Angelic Outreach has gotten several calls from folks declaring that they were in twelfth level Lightbody. We have told them that within this model that can't be so. In this model if you were in twelfth level Lightbody, you wouldn't be able to pick up a telephone because you would be fully in Light and not in this dimension. Now you can have many levels of consciousness and your mind and your consciousness can go many places, but what you are ascending is your physical body and that's why we measure it from there. I knew that if I articulated this model linearly, and in levels, that many of your human egos would involve themselves with, "I'm more evolved than you (or anyone)" games. Please remember that each level is different and essential. No level is "better" than another. Also, as of January 1995, no one on the planet in this parallel reality is in eleventh or twelfth levels of Lightbody.

Finally, we'd like to thank you for being present on the planet at this time. You came here knowing that you would have to go to sleep. You'd have to deny everything that you are, forget everything that you know, and be unrecognizable to yourselves and each other. We have the easy job — we never step away from the Source or experience separation from Spirit. So, we honor you for what you are doing and feel honored to work with you.

— Ariel

What is Lightbody?

All techniques and processes in this book are for Spiritual Light Integration. This is not medical advice. If you are experiencing any of the symptoms mentioned, please see your doctor.

As you probably know, this planet is in a state of ascension. Its frequency is rising at a very rapid rate and it's losing density. Matter, as you know it from the third dimension, is densification of Light. That densification is beginning to drop off and the vibratory rate of each and every one of you, as well as the entire planet, is rising. It's a pretty exciting process.

When you have a process of densification, such as that occurring in your universe, you reach a point when it's gone to maximum separation from the purest forms of Light. At that point of maximum separation, a shift occurs, and the planet begins to reverse its process and start on what we would term a homeward route, i.e. back to the One Point. There are seven to eight million Lightworkers on the planet at this point — what some have called "planetary transition teams." Each one of you is a Lightworker. You are here with special purposes, special skills, and special delights. Many of you are specialists in assisting planets in ascension, having done it thousands and thousands of times.

Each time that a planet ascends, it's a unique process — the process of reunification. And the joy of reunification is expressed differently, depending on how the game was played. This game was one of the greatest possible separation from Spirit you could have. It was very successful.

But the game, as you know it, is now changing. And it began its process of change officially in March 1988. At that point, what we call "activation to first-level Lightbody" occurred for most Lightworkers. That was like a little bell going off in your DNA structure that said, "Yahoo, time to go home!" And it began the process of mutation and change. While this is very joyful most of the time, sometimes it can be a little difficult. But it's a process that all of you have gone through before.

What makes the game interesting is the question, "How should I do it this time? What energies, emotions, and delight will I express in this path of reunification?" What we call the "inbreath and the outbreath" of the Source has occurred many, many times, and this particular inbreath will have its own unique expression and delight, as this planet and all other planets return to the One Point.

This planet is in a state of transition to Light, or a process of ascension. It is a gradual process — you are not matter one day and Light the next day. Everyone is in the process, and many of you are at least halfway.

The Dimensions

First, let me briefly describe the various dimensions or planes of existence in our model. We use a twelve-dimensional model and you, sitting here in a physical body exist in the third dimension: it's matter-based. The fourth dimension is what's called the astral plane: it's basically emotionally-based. Together, these two make up what we call the Lower Creation World. These are the dimensions where the game of separation is carried out. These are the only dimensions in which the illusion of good and evil can be maintained and in which you can feel separated from Spirit and from each other. You've all become quite good at doing that. It's been a very successful game of separation, but now it's time for it to end. So, this planet is in a state of ascension, and is currently vibrating at the lower levels of the astral plane. As part of the ascension process, all of the dimensions will be rolled up into the higher dimensions and will cease to exist.

Because the planet is now vibrating at the level of the mid-astral plane, it's beginning to feel like a dream state, for many of you. You're never quite sure if you are awake or asleep. Continuities are breaking down. There is the feeling that things can change as you hold them in your hand. The pen that you're writing with may become a hammer, and eventually this lack of continuity will no longer bother you, just as it doesn't when you're dreaming. You'll be noticing that your dreamstates are changing, that as you wake up you're not quite sure if you're awake. You will become lucid while you're dreaming, fully conscious in that state. You will be fully self-aware as you move back and forth between different realities, and all of them will feel equally real to you. It won't seem like there is only one true reality, anymore.

The fifth through the ninth dimensions make up the Mid-Creation Realm, in the model that we use. The fifth is the Lightbody dimension, in which you are aware of yourself as a master and a multidimensional being. In the fifth dimension, you are completely spiritually-oriented. Many of you have come in from this plane to be Lightworkers here.

The sixth dimension holds the templates for the DNA patterns of all types of species' creation, including humankind. It's also where the Light languages are stored, and it is made up mostly of color and tone. It is the dimension where consciousness creates through thought, and one of the places where you work during sleep. It can be difficult to get a bead on this, because you're not in a body unless you choose to create one. When you are operating sixth-dimensionally, you are more of an "alive thought." You create through your consciousness, but you don't necessarily have a vehicle for that consciousness.

The seventh dimension is that of pure creativity, pure Light, pure tone, pure geometry, and pure expression. It is a plane of infinite refinement and it is the last plane where you perceive of yourself as "individual."

The eighth is the dimension of group mind or group soul, and is where you would touch base with the vaster part of who you are. It is characterized by loss of sense of the "I." When you travel multidimensionally, this is the plane where you would have the most trouble keeping your consciousness together, because you are pure "we," operating with group goals. So it might seem as though you've gone to sleep or blanked out.

In the model that we use, the ninth dimension is the plane of the collective consciousness of planets, star systems, galaxies, and dimensions. If you visit this dimension, it can be difficult to remain conscious. Once again, it's very difficult to get a sense of "I," because you are so vast that everything is "you." Imagine being the consciousness of a galaxy! Every life-form, every star, planet, and group mind of every species in it is within you.

The tenth through twelfth dimensions make up the Upper Creation Realm. The tenth is the source of the Rays, home of what are called the Elohim. This is where new plans of creation are designed and then sent into the Mid-Creation levels. You can have a sense of "I" at this level, but it won't be at all what you're used to at the third dimension.

The eleventh dimension is that of pre-formed Light — the point before creation and a state of exquisite expectancy, just like the moment before a sneeze or an orgasm. It is the realm of the being known as Metatron, and of Archangels and other Akashics for this Source-system. There are planetary Akashic records and galactic Akashics, as well as the Akashic for an entire Source-system. You are in one Source-system of many. So, we are giving you a description of only one Source-system — this one. If you go to another Source-system, what you will experience will be different. As an Archangel, my home base is the eleventh dimension.

The twelfth dimension is the One Point where all consciousness knows itself to be utterly one with All That Is. There is *no* separation of any kind. If you tap into this level, you know yourself to be completely one with All That Is, with the creator force. If you tap in there, you will never be the same again, because you cannot sustain the same degree of separation if you have experienced complete unity.

Your Bodies

So, in the old world, you have a physical body, and most people's reaction to that physical body is one of it being an enemy, an adversary. After all, it is what you experience karmic limitation through. So most people have this feeling: "If I didn't have a body, I wouldn't be experiencing all this limitation." There can be a total denial that the body itself has a consciousness, and that this consciousness' purpose is to serve you and to serve Spirit. So the physical body walks around most of the time feeling denied and abused, because you say, "Well, I don't want to experience karma through you and therefore I'm not going to pay any attention to what you tell me. I'm not going to feed you what you want to eat. I'm not going to let you play in any way that you want to play." You do all these odd things to your bodies. If you think about it, most of you have a love/hate relationship with your body. "It's too fat, it's too tall, it's too wide, it's too bald, it's too curly, it's too long, it's too short." So, most of you have this sort of relationship with the physical.

You also have something which we call an etheric blueprint. And most of you, if you perceive on an etheric level, perceive this body at about a half-inch away from your skin. It also exists within you. This body holds structures that are seventh-, sixth-, fifth-, and fourth-dimensional. Now, we're going to explain that. We're talking in terms of dimensions. You are currently in the third dimension. The fourth dimension in our model is the astral level. This is where the majority of your karmic patterning is stored within the etheric body. It sets up the motions that go on in the other energy bodies, which bring you karmic experiences. It also works to keep your DNA functioning at limited, survival-based levels by inhibiting the amount of Light your physical body can absorb.

Then you have the fifth-dimensional Lightbody structure (which lies dormant), and in that structure are something we call etheric crystals. These crystals block certain flows and prevent that body from activating too early.

The fifth-dimensional etheric blueprint is made up of an axiotonal meridian system, an axial circulatory system, and spin points through which these systems and structures are connected.

As part of this game of separation, the human axiotonal meridians were cut off from direct connection with the Overself and other star populations. This created brain atrophy, aging, and death. Axiotonal lines are the equivalent of acupuncture meridians that can connect with the Oversoul and resonant star systems.

Through the axiotonal lines, a human body is directly repro-grammed by the Overself into a new body of Light. Axiotonal lines exist independently of any physical body or biological form. They emanate from various star systems and are the means by which the galactic body controls its renewing mechanisms. Picture the Milky Way as the body of a living conscious being. The stars and planets are organs in that body; all the different species on the stars and planets are like cells in the organs of the galactic body, renewing the energies of the organs and cells. Planet Earth and her inhabitants were separated from the galactic body and the Oversoul to play this game of separation, and are now being reconnected.

The axiotonal lines are made of Light and Sound. The functions of the Office of the Christ are necessary to restructure the axiotonal meridians in the human body. Once reconnection has occurred, the Overself transmits the appropriate color/tone frequencies to regen-erate the physical body into a Lightbody.

The axiotonal lines lie along the acupuncture meridians and con-nect into some of them by means of the "spin points." Spin points are small spherical vortexes of electromagnetic energy that feel like they are on the skin surface. There are also spin points in every cell of the body. These cellular points emit Sound and Light frequencies which spin the atoms of the molecules in the cell at a faster rate. Through the increased molecular spin, Light fibers are created which set up a grid for cellular regeneration.

The axial circulatory system was completely vestigial in the human species, due to the axiotonal lines being disconnected so that this game could be played. It is a fifth-dimensional energy system that connects the spin points on the skin surface to every spin point in every cell. It is a model for physical transmutation and it is being renewed now that the axiotonal lines are reconnected. The axial system pulses energy like the circulatory system pulses blood, but the axial system is basically electrical in nature, like the nervous system. The Overself sends energy into the axiotonal line, which then goes into the spin points on the surface of the skin, feeding the physical acu-puncture meridians and then the axial system. As the axial system receives energy from the Overself, it recombines color and sound to realign the blood, lymph, endocrine, and nervous systems into the Divine Template, the Adam Kadmon. It also carries the energy from the Overself into the spin points inside the cells. This stimulates the spin points to emit Sound and Light to create a gridwork for the renewed evolution of humankind.

The sixth-dimensional structure holds templates, or patterns, that are set for the formation of matter and Lightbodies. It is where the entire DNA encodement is held. So you have this sixth-dimensional template that determines what is in your DNA and the shape of your physical form. Lightworkers carry bits of genetic material from the various species which live on the 383 ascending planets.

The seventh-dimensional structures are for embodiment of Divinity. They act as an interface between the physical or astral bodies of a given species and its Divine blueprint. The Adam Kadmon is the Divine form from which all sentient species forms emanate; therefore it is inclusive of myriad forms. The seventh-dimensional structures are very flexible, differing from individual to individual. Preset "thresh-olds" within the structure and within the third- or fourth-dimensional bodies create a ceiling on how much the Oversouls can interface with and embody in any given species.

So, before activation of the bodies to Light, if you were walking around this planet, you were mostly aware of the fourth-dimensional patterning in your bodies.

The next body in this model is what we call the emotional body. The emotional body, the mental body, and the spiritual bodies are made up of double tetrahedrons, if you look at them fifth-dimensionally. They have certain specific rates of spin. In the emotional body, you have all of these wonderful stuck places, and all they are is geometry that happens not to be moving in a coherent fashion. That incoherent motion is caused by the fourth-dimensional structures in the etheric blueprint. So, you sit on emotion — that's part of the karma game.

In this game, you are taught to not express. Expressing is dangerous. If you cannot express, you will lock down those wonderful geometries in that field. What happens is you bop along until you run into someone with a complementary "stuck-point." Your little geometries lock and there you are, doing a karma. You're stuck. And you're stuck until it is complete and they get themselves unjammed. You experience this as limitation. You experience this as discomfort. And you experience this as "Why the hell am I here?"

The mental body is also made of geometries. This body's function is to determine your reality. It believes that it's in control. It believes that it is running the show. It isn't, but its whole job is to determine what is "real." It determines how the universe recreates itself in your life. So, by determining what's real, it keeps you stuck in the karma game. There is nothing the mental body hates more than change. Nothing. Because if you change what you're doing now, you may not survive in the future. It keeps maintaining a reality that it thinks will keep you alive, whether it works or not. It doesn't give a flying fig over whether you're happy or satisfied in any way. It is set there to maintain.

The natural state of All That Is is unified within itself. The amount of energy it takes to maintain the illusion of separation is absolutely incredible. It takes so much more energy than to simply let go. That's part of the reason why the mental body was developed to be so strong. The easiest way to maintain the illusion of separation was to have the mental body declare everything it cannot see as "not real." So it screens out all the impulses coming from your Spirit.

The spiritual body (the next one out) is also made of the same double tetrahedrons, and is — for the most part — ignored in a karma game. Its original design is to connect you to your Oversoul, your Christ Oversoul, and to the I AM Presence. Obviously, the spiritual body is underused in a karma game. It just sits out there and those connections are not made.

The spiritual body brings through impulses and information from your own Spirit, which then hit up against a mental body that says,

"That's not real." When the emotional body picks up hints from Spirit, instead of trying to express them, it shuts down. And you keep repeating this entire cycle of limitation and separation, because this entire game was based on the illusion of separation from Spirit. That's what it was all about.

Your Chakras

The other things that shift function are your chakra systems. Most of you are aware of chakras. You have a total of fourteen major chakras that exist multidimensionally — seven within your physical body, seven outside your body — plus the Alpha and Omega "chakras." Most people see or feel chakras as radiant, spinning energy sources, but chakras also have a sixth-dimensional internal structure.

Under the karma game, the structure of the seven embodied chakras was deliberately limited so that they could only transduce energy from the astral plane. They were "sealed." With this limited blueprint, a chakra looks like two cones. One of the cones opens out towards the front of the body; the other one opens out towards the back. Where their narrowed points touch in the center of the body, they are "sealed" so that they remain in this configuration. This narrow part in the center tends to be clogged with mental and emotional "debris," causing the spin of the cones to slow down or stop. This starves the acupuncture meridian system of energy and can cause illness or death. This type of chakra structure can only move energy front to back or back to front, and cannot utilize higher-dimensional frequencies.

When the Lightbody process is activated, the "seals" in the center points are broken. The chakra structure gradually opens up from the center until the chakra is spherical in shape. This allows the chakra to radiate energy in all directions and begin to transduce frequencies from the higher dimensions. The body sheds the collected karmic debris and the spherical blueprint makes it impossible for any more to collect. The spheres keep expanding in size, until all the chakras merge as one unified energy field. Each of the upper chakras (the non-embodied chakras) have a different geometric blueprint structure, one that is appropriate for transducing the specific dimensional or Oversoul frequencies associated with the chakra. The eighth and eleventh chakras also contain flat crystalline templates that the galactic axiotonal lines pass through. These templates are used by the Oversoul to modulate the star influences on one's physical body, once one's axiotonal meridians are reconnected. The Oversoul recalibrates the axiotonal lines and the axial circulatory system through the eighth chakra. Therefore, the eighth chakra acts as the "master control" for the mutation of the body's systems and the merging of the energy bodies.

Until recently, the Alpha and Omega "chakras" have been vestigial in the human body type. Even though the Alpha and Omega "chakras" are energy centers, they have a completely different type of blueprint and function than that of the other chakras. They are finely tuned energy regulators for electric, magnetic, and gravitational waves, as well as serving as anchors for the seventh-dimensional etheric blueprint.

The Alpha "chakra" is six to eight inches above and about two inches forward from the center of your head. It connects you to your immortal body of Light in the fifth dimension. The Omega "chakra" is about eight inches below the end of your spine and connects you to the planet as a hologram, as well as to your entire holographic grid of incarnations. Unlike the fourth-dimensional karmic matrix, this is a completely non-karmic type of connection. The eighth chakra is seven to nine inches above the exact center of the head, above the Alpha "chakra." There is a column of Light, about four inches in diameter, that extends from your eighth chakra down through the center of your body, through the embodied chakras, to about eight inches below your feet. This column supports a tube of Light, about one and three-quarters inches in diameter, which runs down the exact center of the entire length of the column.

When the Alpha and Omega "chakras" are open and operating correctly, you will experience something called the Waves of Metatron, moving through the inner column of Light. These magnetic, electric, and gravitational waves oscillate back and forth between the Alpha and Omega "chakras," which regulate the waves' amplitude and frequency. These waves stimulate and support the flow of pranic life force energy in the smaller tube of Light. The Waves of Metatron also assist in coordinating the physical body's mutation to the pre-existing template of your immortal body of Light.

As the embodied chakras open into their spherical structure, grids are laid down which connect the chakras directly into spin points on the skin's surface, thereby connecting the chakras directly into the new axiotonal and axial systems. By connecting the chakra grids into the axiotonal lines, the chakras are hooked up into higher evolutionary, universal resonance grids and wave motions. This assists the chakras and the emotional, mental, and spiritual bodies to merge into one unified energy field. This unified field then receives the Oversoul bodies and moves in synchrony with universal waves and pulses. This whole new system then transmits these waves and pulses through the spin points, into the axial circulatory system, to recalibrate the pulses and flows of bodily fluids.

Now, in a karma game, since you are in a state of separation from Spirit and living in a state of limitation and you're alienated from your physical body, that usually means that you're not in your body. If you are not in your body, you cannot activate the heart chakra.

If you cannot activate your heart chakra, the chakras which are operating predominantly are the base chakra, the navel chakra and the solar plexus chakra. All of your interactions are coming out of instinctive terror, karmic patterning, power, lust, greed, or sheer ego-centered power interactions with people. So you don't get to have a higher interaction until you are fully in your body. And, of course, the upper, non-embodied chakras are not activated at all.

Activation

In March 1988, all of what we call Lightworkers were activated to at least first-level Lightbody on this planet. On April 16, 1989, the entire crystalline structure of matter and every inhabitant on this planet was activated to third-level Lightbody. Now, this is not an optional process; everyone is experiencing this. Lots of people are leaving the planet because they don't want to do this in this lifetime. You can choose to do this process in any lifetime you have ever had, in any parallel reality. So, don't feel that we're losing people. It's OK. They're just not prepared to do it in *this* incarnation.

First Level of Lightbody

So, you have had an activation to the first level of Lightbody. Now when this happened — for most of you — it was as though a lightbulb went off in your DNA: "It's time to go home." That's what it feels like in the body: "It's time to go home." And there's a sense of elation that comes up from the body that's just wonderful. At the same time, the body said: "Time to drop density" and most of you had a very good bout of the "flu." Much of what's going around right now that people are calling the "flu," we call "mutational symptoms." When your body drops density, it will tend to have headaches, vomiting, diarrhea, acne, rashes, anything that is a flu-like symptom — muscle aches, joint aches are very common. And if you remember back to March 1988, there was a "flu" epidemic: it was a Light epidemic!

Current human genetic science has called 99% of the DNA "junk," because "we don't know what it all means." In fact, human DNA holds bits of genetic material from every species on Earth, plus genetic material holographically encoded with the collective experience of all of humanity and the experiences of your holographic grid of incarnations, as well as bits of genetic encoding from the sentient species of 383 ascending planets across five local universes! Your DNA also holds latent encodements for mutating your physical body into a

Lightbody.

Only about 7% of the genetic encodements were active before March 1988. Then, in the first level of Lightbody, Spirit activated a series of these latent encodements by infusing a tone/color sequence. These newly activated encodements signalled your body to begin a mutational change in the DNA and a profound alteration in the way your cells metabolize energy.

We measure Lightbody levels by the ability of your cells to metabolize Light. The marker for this new cellular activity is the amount of adenosine triphosphate (ATP) in the cells. Before Lightbody activation, the energy for cellular functioning came from an energy production and storage system which shuttles energy back and forth between adenosine *di*phosphate (ADP) and adenosine *tri*phosphate. ATP is an energy storage compound found in the cells. Within the mitochondria, food is converted into energy for the cells, which is then bound up in the ATP. ATP has a chain of three phosphate groups, which projects out from the molecule. When an ATP molecule loses its outermost phosphate group, it becomes an ADP molecule. The breaking of the chemical bond releases energy for the cell to carry out its functions, such as creating proteins. ADP can again become ATP by picking up some energy and a phosphate group. ATP and ADP lose and gain phosphate groups to release and store energy for cellular functioning. This is a closed system of biological energy, ensuring aging and death. No new energy is gained.

When the Lightbody mutation was activated, a series of latent DNA encodements lit up and began to give new directives to the cells. One of the first instructions was to tell the cells to recognize Light as a new energy source. At first, the cellular consciousness didn't know what to do with this information. As the cells were bathed in Light, the mitochondria (which are very Light sensitive) began to fully absorb this new color/tonal activation and produce lots of ATP, in bursts. The cells had not yet absorbed enough Light to stabilize the phosphate bond, so the ATP broke down very rapidly into ADP, and cellular metabolism was dramatically speeded up. Accumulated toxins, old traumas, and stored thoughts and emotions began to flush from the physical body and created flu-like symptoms.

The physical form in its old manner has separated brain function-ing into right and left hemisphere functions. Also, the pineal and pituitary glands are atrophied — about the size of a pea rather than the size of a walnut. On activation, brain chemistry begins to change and to produce new synapses.

Second Level of Lightbody

In the second level, the sixth-dimensional etheric blueprint begins to be flooded with Light and it begins to release the fourth-dimensional structures which tie you into karmic experiences across all lifetimes. As a result, you may have begun to feel a little disoriented, along with having had more bouts of "the flu."

You probably will have found yourself lying in bed, saying "Why am I here?", "Who am I?", and might have gotten an inkling that there was something called "Spirit" in your life. Now we'll also define another term. When we use the term "soul," we are talking about the differentiated part of Spirit that experiences through your physi-cal body. When we talk in terms of Spirit, we are talking about that part of you which is undifferentiated and totally connected to the Source.

So, in the second level of Lightbody, you are releasing fourth-dimensional structures which begin to change the spin in the geom-etries of your emotional, mental, and spiritual bodies. You are begin-ning to change very rapidly. Most of what you're experiencing is strictly physical. You may feel very tired.

Third Level of Lightbody

In the third level of Lightbody, your physical senses become out-rageously strong. The example we use is that the smell of that old piece of garbage stuck in the garbage disposal is driving you crazy — from upstairs. Everything may seem incredibly tactile. The chair you're sitting on or the clothes you're wearing may be terribly distracting because they feel so sensual. Often, people rediscover the joy of sex in third-level Lightbody. That's why there has been a rise in pregnancies and births since April 1989, when the planet and her population were activated to the third level.

Everything that is happening is very centered in the physical body. It's beginning to open up into what we call a "bio-transducer system." Your body was designed to decode and work with Higher Light energies as well as transmit these energies to the planet. As part of the game of separation, these functions atrophied. The magnification of the physical senses is the first sign of the awakening of your body as a "bio-transducer."

Undifferentiated Light from the Oversoul pours into the fifth-dimensional axiotonal lines. From the axiotonal spin point interfaces on the skin surface, the fifth-dimensional axial circulatory system begins to form. The axial system then extends into and activates the spin points in every cell of the physical body.

Whereas in the first and second levels of Lightbody, the physical body was being bathed in Light, now — in the third level — each cell has Light focused directly into it through the axial system.

The mitochondria usually recognize this Light as "food," and produce more ATP. Because the cell is receiving Light as usable energy, less of the ATP turns into ADP. As the axial system feeds energy from the Oversoul into the cellular spin points, the spin points produce Sound and Light frequencies which change the atomic spin of the cells' molecules, especially in the hydrogen atoms. As the atomic spin in the ATP molecule increases, a new functioning emerges. The three phosphate groups forming the stalk of the ATP molecule begin to act like an antenna for undifferentiated Light, and the symmetrical head of the molecule acts like a prism, breaking down the Light into subtle color spectrums, usable by the dormant DNA encodements.

Before Lightbody was activated, the ribonucleic acid (RNA) in the cells acted as a one-way messenger. It carried directives from the active 7% of the DNA to other parts of the cell for execution, such as what proteins to synthesize. In third-level Lightbody, the RNA became a two-way messenger! Now it took Light, broken down into usable color frequencies by the ATP antenna/prism, back into the DNA strands. The dormant genetic encodements gradually awaken with each successive Lightbody level and give their information to the RNA, which transmits it to the rest of the cell.

It's much like the new CD laser technologies on Earth. An enormous amount of information can be stored on one disk. Imagine that a vast amount of information can be stored in a color range of red and vast amounts of data can be stored in a blue spectrum. A red laser beam is run across the disk and all the red information is now able to be read, but you still know nothing about what is stored in the blue spectrum. You run a blue laser beam over the CD and now all of that data is available. The Light/color frequencies "read" the DNA in much the same way. Until the color spectrum is transmitted, you have no idea what's in there. Each Lightbody level has its own color/tonal signature. In this way, Spirit achieves the gradual mutation of the physical body.

The one-way DNA-to-RNA information transfer and the ATP-ADP energy cycle were closed systems, ensuring entropy. Nothing could change, except to decay. With Lightbody activation, new, fully open systems can develop, making infinite energy and infinite information available to the body. A dialogue between your physical body and Spirit has begun.

In the first two levels of Lightbody, you can still reverse the entire process because the ATP and RNA have not gained this new functioning. At the third level of Lightbody, it is a continuing mutation that you cannot stop. That's why when the indigenous population of this planet and the planet herself were activated, they were activated to the third level of Lightbody: so the process couldn't be messed with, quite simply.

Also, in that activation to the third level of Lightbody, a set point was created between this planet and all the other planets that are ascending out of the physical plane, so that you're all in synch. It isn't just that this planet is ascending; the entire dimension is ascending! And so is the entire astral plane. There will be no more physical and astral planes when this is done. This entire process is something we call an "inbreath" of the Source.

In our model, the Source (the One Point, All That Is, or God) manifests as inbreaths and outbreaths of creativity — very slow outbreaths and very quick inbreaths. A Lightworker once asked us why it takes billions of years to densify a game to this level of separation and yet we're turning the whole game around in twenty years. Imagine that you are the One, and You decide to explore the myriad possible facets of what You are through levels of progressive individuation. It's like stretching a rubber band. As you achieve more and more individuation, the rubber band gets tighter and tighter and tighter. Well, there's a point when it has stretched as far as it can. You have separated the maximum that You can from Your Oneness and the tension is tremendous. So, You turn around and let go of the rubber band — your separateness. What happens? You shoot back to Your Oneness very quickly.

On this planet, you have a game of separation that has now completed every possible permutation of relationship and interaction you can have. Every karmic relationship that you can explore has been explored and when that happens, you begin the "inbreath." This game is over. It's time to go home.

What we term "Lightworkers" are people who are here as transition teams to assist in this process of Light. That's why you're here. Some of you have been here for the entire cycle. Some of you are assisting in setting up this particular game and have decided to stay and see how it would work. If you were to look at time linearly, you're sitting out across linear time and across all parallel times, activating, turning into Light. A planet does not ascend in an instant — it ascends from the moment of its creation. And that's why so many of you took on so many lifetimes here. Others of you are showing up to assist now, and that's OK, too.

Fourth Level of Lightbody

As you transition into the fourth level of Lightbody, you begin to go into what we call the mental stages. This begins a massive change in your brain chemistry and the electromagnetics of your brain. At this point, if you have regulator crystals in your etheric body, they may become very uncomfortable. You may start having cluster headaches, seizures, chest pains, blurry vision, or your hearing may go out.

These crystals keep lines of Light within the fifth-dimensional blueprint from making connections, just like electricity. Chest pains are something you may experience throughout the Lightbody process, because your heart begins to open at deeper and deeper levels. Your entire vision and hearing apparatus begins to alter, as parts of the brain open up. A whole different functioning starts in at that fourth level of Lightbody. The hemispheres of the brain want to begin to start firing across both hemispheres at the same time, and if there is something stopping that, it can feel really yucky. Most people begin to feel some electrical stuff going on in their head. You may literally feel electrical energy running across your scalp or down your spine.

You may have your first taste of non-linear thinking, which can be either delightful or terrifying. You begin to go through a mental shift. The mental body is beginning to say to itself, "Gee whiz. Maybe I'm not running the show."

Usually about the fourth level of Lightbody, someone shows up in your life saying "The prime directive is to follow your Spirit without hesitation," or something similar. Suddenly the mental body gets the idea: "Gee, maybe something else is in control of this because I'm sure not!" And it begins to shift how it views itself and begins to get a little uncertain about what's real and what's not. Your Spirit begins to put through much wider, vaster pictures of reality or patterning through your energy bodies.

In the fourth level, you get the inkling that there is a Spirit. Suddenly, you get impulses from areas you didn't before and you're thinking that maybe you should start following those impulses. Your mental body is screaming: "Wait a minute. What is this?" It starts trying to retain control over the world and it's pretty uncomfortable because it's getting an inkling that everything is changing. Everything it has defined as real is beginning to shift.

You may have flashes of telepathy or clairvoyance. Just about everybody gets empathy right around this time. And once again, the mental body tries to clamp down because it feels like the emotional body is opening and, of course, that's dangerous and it's going to get you killed, according to mental body rules. So the flashes of empathy can be very uncomfortable for people and yet at the same time, it's exhilarating because you feel so much more connection with everything, a sense of "I'm connected to things here. There are people here that maybe I've known before. I know you from somewhere. Gee, you look familiar." And you begin to get an inkling that maybe there's a purpose to your being here.

Fifth Level of Lightbody

At the fifth level of Lightbody, usually the mental body says "Maybe I'll try to follow Spirit. I don't know if I buy it, but maybe I'll try it." And it starts that process of looking for clues.

A person often begins to have some flashes of themselves doing other things. Often, your dream sequencing begins to change. You begin to remember a little more of your dreams. Some people open up to lucid dreaming in the fifth level.

At some points a person can feel like they might be going crazy, because they may be beginning to experience non-linear thought processes. Suddenly, rather than having to look at something in this nice set fashion, they are cognizant of the whole, i.e., non-linear thinking. And then the mental body says, "Wait a minute, I can't control this. Can we survive and do this?" So, it is questioning what is happening: "Is there a Spirit? I think there's a Spirit. I better figure out whether there's a Spirit because otherwise, we're all going to die." You get a lot of the survival patterning coming up out of the mental body. So the mental body begins to shift the way it moves and it begins to drop patterning out.

A part of you is just like a little child saying, "Yeah, we're going to Light. Yeah, we're going to Light." And you're so happy. And then you have the mental body, just an old grump. And you get to see the two halves of yourself: "Wow! I get to make a decision here about what I want to do."

You begin to become aware that you are more than you thought you were. When that happens, the mental body says, "Oh no, we're not!" and slams down, but then it opens up again. So you keep going through this process of feeling like you're opening and closing, opening and closing. It can feel a little manic-depressive. What your Spirit needs you to do is to get your mental body to surrender its control so that you can become an active embodied Spirit on this planet, fully conscious on every dimension.

Also, in the fifth level of Lightbody, you begin to become aware that a lot of your pictures about the way things are aren't yours. You begin to be aware that, "Oh dear, I'm doing that just like my father. My father was picky and I'm acting just like him. Wait a minute, that's not my energy." Or, "My child just knocked over the milk and I'm screaming at her just like my mother screamed at me. That's not my energy. I don't want to be doing this. This is not what I want to be doing here."

You become aware that you contain entire pictures of reality that are not yours. And you begin the mental sorting out process of "Who am I," as different from those around you. Everyone holds, within their energy fields, the entire picture of "the way things are" from their parents, grandparents, siblings, and lovers. The entire picture is updated continuously. As you become aware that these structures are contained in your fields, you can feel very closed in by them.

Because here you are — you can feel all this change going on in your body, all this wonderful stuff, and at the same time, you feel like you are in a glass cage — all this change and you are so contained by these pictures. So you start that sorting out process: "Well, I'll take some of this, I'll take none of that, a little of that and a little of this."

And you begin to become more and more aware of your energy. What is truly yours. When you have a thought or a picture about something, you just ask yourself, "Am I just running my father, or is this me?" It can be a little scary to someone, when they first look in the mirror and they say, "Oh no, I really am turning into my mother. I swore I would not turn into my mother." But you find that you get to a point where those pictures of reality begin to shift out of your fields.

Sixth Level of Lightbody

In the sixth level of Lightbody you are actively, consciously shifting reality pictures out of your field. At this time, your Spirit is usually putting you into contact with people who are working with the Lightbody process. Maybe Spirit is throwing books at you off of shelves. Have you had this experience of being in a book store and having books fall at you? You may have those at any time. It's one of the favorite ways for Spirit to say, "Read this." You begin to get other information, other pictures of reality. You begin to take in vaster understandings of your own reality and how you operate in them.

Often, in the fifth and sixth levels, you have experiences of things not being solid. In your meditation, you may look down and sense that your hand is not solid, or you have one of those odd experiences where you put your hand against a wall and you feel the wall give. So you may be having flashes of multidimensionality. You may be having flashes of non-linear thinking and feeling like nothing is real. This can be a real shock for you mental-body types out there who want everything all laid out in nice little lines — suddenly you see the whole picture at once. Then you have to go back and make up how you got there. Some of you experience this extensively. The mental body begins to cognate very differently.

A lot of people leave the planet in sixth level Lightbody, because it's extremely uncomfortable for most of them. "Do I want to be here? Do I want to look at all this stuff? Do I want to be part of this process?" A lot of people opt out. That's okay. They are doing this process in another life. They don't have to do it in all of them. Generally, if we can assist someone to survive the fifth and sixth levels, they're home free. If they choose to not opt out of the planet at that point, they will usually stay and work with the entire process.

Be kind to your fellow human beings. This is a very painful stage because this is the stage where the entire sense of identity is restructured. When you run into people on the street, and many of you will, you may be asked, "What are you doing? You look so wonderful." Give them the information that the planet is going to Light, that we are in an ascension process. "If you want to know more about it, here are some good books you could read. Here are some people you could go see. If you need to talk about it, here is my number." Support those around you.

Usually at the sixth level of Lightbody, you go through a re-evaluative state that is extremely uncomfortable. "Do I want to be here? Do I want to live? Do I want to play?" It can be pretty severe. You hate your job, you hate your life, you hate everybody and everything all at once.

In the sixth level, you find that lots of people begin to leave your life. This is the time when you're likely to change your job, get married, stop being married — all your friends may change, your entire sense of purpose changes and there's a sense of learning to not be afraid of change. If you freeze up, this level can last for up to a year and be very miserable. But most people learn fairly quickly to relax and let everything flow around them.

New people come into your life who are far more in alignment with what you're here to do than you've ever had before. You're all here in work groups — those people you're here to work with. This clearing away of those in your life who are there for karma or out of a sense of obligation can be a little bit scary. But, if you take a deep breath and say "I wish you well and have a nice life. I'll see you next time," you'll find that the people you're here to be with will quickly come into your life. This "amps up" the whole thing and it begins to be fun.

Usually between the sixth and seventh level of Lightbody, you experience what we call a descension of Spirit. This means that a vaster part of who you are in the upper dimensions comes to reside in your body. That shifts everything around.

You feel like you've come through a tunnel. You've come from a place of "Maybe there's a Spirit and maybe I'll try to follow it" to "I know, within every cell of my being, that I am Spirit in action on this planet." And you begin what we call the emotional transition to learning to be the vastness of Spirit. About one-third of the Lightbody structure is now lit up in the etheric blueprint. Many times you may experience yourself as radiating light, which is pretty exciting. Most of the time in the seventh level of Lightbody, people's eyes change. You begin to see a deeper level of Light coming out of people's eyes.

You and those around you are beginning to cognate in a non-linear way and you begin to get flashes of telepathy. You begin to get flashes of communication on levels that you communicate on all the time but are unaware of. You have always been telepathic. You have always been clairvoyant. You've always been multidimensional. But your mental body and brain have been screening it out and away from you. So, the screens are dropping and you begin to recognize what's been there all along. Things begin to feel normal. There's a point where it's no longer a big "A-ah." It's not the lightbulb going off anymore. It's just "I am here. I am. I am fully here, now." You become a delightful dance that you play with your Spirit.

The entire planet and its population appears to be doing a strong re-evaluation. The polarization of energies is happening at more and more heightened levels. It's almost like the volume is being turned up. Planetary polarization is becoming more and more intense. You'll find that those of you who are beginning to live Heaven on Earth, will exist side by side with those who are experiencing Hell on Earth.

I wish to remind you that all beings are vast multidimensional Divine Masters.

We ask that you learn compassion, and compassion is not being co-dependent: "Oh, let me take care of you!" Compassion is being willing to do whatever is necessary to assist someone in taking their next higher step. That occasionally means kicking someone's feet out from under them; that occasionally means being a wake-up call; that occasionally means calling someone on their "stuff"; and it often means loving them for their wholeness, their totality, the parts of them that are awake as well as the parts of them that are asleep. Remember they go into sleep with the first part of the Mission. Honor those who have slept well. Many Lightworkers have a fear of people who are asleep built into them. Begin to dismantle that particular piece of enemy patterning. You will naturally evolve it into a sense of service to Spirit and a service to all life. It will be ecstatic. But understand how difficult this period was and is for many people. Look at the level of re-evaluation, and you'll understand why we call this level the one that determines whether someone will do this process or not. This is the place where a lot of people must bail out or get with the program.

Seventh Level of Lightbody

In the seventh level of Lightbody, you begin to enter the emotional stages of Lightbody: focusing on deeper and deeper levels of opening in the heart chakra. As you open into the heart, a feeling of connection with the planet opens up: that feeling of falling in love with this planet, feeling like "If I don't hug that tree, I just can't make it. I have to hug that tree." There's a playfulness that begins to open up at the seventh level of Lightbody. You become a little more childlike in the way you operate.

At this point, if you've got blocks in the emotional body, they really begin to come up, because as you move toward expressing your divinity and your vastness, anything that blocks that vastness begins to release. Some of it's fun; some of it's not. It depends on how much of a stranglehold the mental body wants to keep. If the mental body is in sync, the release is usually quick and easy.

You may find that you become far more emotional than ever before, and as you move through these levels, you find that your emotions become like a child's: when you're sad, you cry; when you're angry, you yell; when you're happy, you laugh. You express ecstasy.

You express whatever emotion is flowing through your emotional body in that moment. You begin to operate in the NOW far more than ever before. You see, in the karma game, your mental body lives in the future: it's always living in "what if"s. The emotional body lives in the past, triggered by what you've experienced before. So, you rarely experience exactly what's happening in front of you. In the seventh level of Lightbody, you begin to experience NOW. Enough synchronization has happened among your fields that you have begun to have long stretches of being fully in the present — and it feels really good.

As the emotional body drops all of its old patterning, it may mean that you have to complete your relationships with a lot of people. Having dropped all those pictures of reality out of the mental body, and now dropping the emotional attachments out of the emotional body means that your relationships with other people begin to change very quickly. In the seventh, eighth, and ninth levels of Lightbody, your personal relationships turn into something we call "transpersonal." That means they are not based on emotional attachment; they become based in whether your Spirit is guiding you to be with that person at any given time. It's a very different way of relating.

By the time someone is in the ninth level of Lightbody, they are usually operating this way most of the time. Sometimes, you may seem "cold" to people, because you don't have the emotional hooks and there is no intensity. "I can't manipulate you. I can't hook into you." People can get very upset. This is a natural part of the Lightbody process, as you shift from being in karmic relations into non-karmic, Spirit-based relationships.

In seventh-level Lightbody, the heart chakra opens to a much deeper functioning than it ever has before. Many people experience chest pains; it's probably not angina. It doesn't feel the same as a heart attack, because it feels like it's in the center of your body, radiating outward. It's an opening of the heart chakra gateway. If you're in a meditative state and you want to go multidimensional, you can go right through your own heart chakra.

On this planet, the heart chakra has a membrane in it, which we call the Gates of Eden. You all know that lovely story about Adam and Eve being cast out of the Gates of Eden, and there is an angel with a flaming sword so that they cannot reenter. What that is is a membrane in the heart chakra that prevents you from going multidimensional. It means that it keeps this game contained. None of the stuff that happens on the physical plane can get above the astral plane, so it can't affect anything else. Part of the way you do that is to close part of the heart chakra, so that you can't have multidimensional experience. That membrane is opened now, in everyone on the planet. The heart chakra shifts its functioning and it begins to open into deeper and deeper levels. You can travel into any dimension through the heart chakra: it is all contained within you. The heart chakra shifts functioning and begins to take predominance over the other chakras.

The way most chakras are portrayed is that they are conical, narrowing in the center, and spinning. Well, they are mutating, too. First they become spherical-shaped and they radiate in all directions at once. Then, if the heart chakra takes predominance, it all begins to open up and the chakra system merges into what we call the unified chakra. It's a unified energy field. It feels wonderful. When you do something like the Unified Chakra meditation, you assist your Lightbody process.

Assisting that chakra merger also assists those energy bodies — the emotional, mental, and spiritual bodies — to begin to merge. They merge into a unified field. In the seventh level of Lightbody, those chakras are kicking into merged states that they haven't been in before. And you begin to become aware that when you have survival fears coming up, or you have blocked emotions, all it means is that these fields have stepped out of unity. It's an illusion, even though it feels real. All you have to do is realign and re-merge the bodies, and the fear drops away.

The chakra unification is really important for your growth into Lightbody, because it allows you to handle any amount of energy (no matter how vast) through the physical form, without any damage:

the entire field holds it. You'll have points when you'll tap into a vaster part of yourself and, if your chakras aren't moving in a unified fashion, you will feel as if you've stuck your finger into an electrical outlet. It's like you only have wiring for 20 volts but you just had 400 put through your body. When you utilize the unified chakra, you don't have that happen anymore; you can handle it at all levels.

The pineal and pituitary glands begin to open up in the seventh level of Lightbody, and you may experience a pressure on your forehead or at the back of your head.

When the pituitary gland is functioning at its higher level, you will not age or die. So very often, about seventh-level Lightbody, people start to look really young. Their whole energy changes around their face and lines drop out. The pineal operates in a multidimensional way. One of the things reported is the sensation of an ice pick, of sharp pain right in the top of the head. Most of you have heard of something called the third eye. Well, there is something called the fourth eye, just at the top of your head; it's your multidimensional sight. It's located where the soft spot is, the place that doesn't harden all the way in most of you. For some of you, that eye opens easily; it's just your multidimensional sight and it just does it when it's time. For others of you, it can feel like it's trying to open, but it's hitting up against something. It may be a structure placed within the etheric body. As that's removed, you'll find this eye opens up.

You begin to have these rather odd experiences. You may begin to be aware of yourself in other dimensions or aware of yourself in other bodies on the planet, which is grand fun. We call those concurrents. Most of you have twelve of you, in other bodies in this parallel reality, on this planet right now, living vastly different lives than you may be living now. You become a little more aware of yourself in other bodies. At first when this happens, people think they are remembering past lives, and they might be. But more often they are usually aware of themselves in the same parallel reality. A lot of you have some incarnations in dolphin and whale bodies. So you may have flashes of being in water or a fluidity of motion through and around your body that you've not normally had in a human form. Of course, the dolphins and whales are other individually ensouled species on this planet. They are Lightworkers too. They set up the group mind grids for this planet.

In seventh-level Lightbody, most beings are operating pretty much fourth-dimensionally in their consciousness: "Not only am I going to ascend tomorrow, but I am going to heal this planet. I am single-handedly going to save this planet and all you poor dummies out there. I'm going to do it. I'm going to drag you all to Light. I'm going to protect you from yourself and save you from your karma. And I'm going to save you from the dark forces." Beings in seventh-level Lightbody usually have an identity of being a healer, or an awakener, or a person who saves themselves, others, or the planet. Actually, they are doing karmic monads. It takes a little bit to realize that so many parts of you are still existing in duality. You may be requiring that the planet or people be sick so you can heal them, or lost so you can save them, or asleep so that they can be awakened. It requires that people not be fully functional.

In the seventh level, you are developing the knowing that all beings are vast multidimensional masters. They may be masters who are exploring divinity or they may be masters who are exploring limitation, but they are masters nonetheless. Everyone is doing exactly what they wish to be doing and they are fine. If a person has led a life where they have been constantly protecting and taking care of everyone around them, this is a deeply freeing revelation. Then it becomes okay to simply allow them their process.

This is a time where most beings run an amazing amount of what's called spiritual significance and spiritual ambition. In the physical body, pictures of reality about being completely separate from God are held in deep states of shame or guilt. When people begin to access who they are multidimensionally and they haven't integrated the physical body, they try to deny its pictures of reality. Beings will often adopt spiritual forms and rules. They try to say, wear, and do all the "right" spiritual things, eat all the "right" foods, and suppress or deny any part of themselves or others that doesn't fit their ideals. The mental body is accustomed to following forms and rules. It's trying very hard to find a form for following Spirit.

Spiritual significance is a mental body defense mechanism against feelings of shame and unworthiness held in the physical body. "I'm spiritually advanced (and you're not). I'm one of the 144,000 rainbow warriors (and you're not). I'm going to ascend next Saturday (and you're not). I'm going to heaven (and you're not)." Spiritual significance is by its nature exclusionary.

Spiritual ambition is a mental body defense against feelings of guilt and incompetence held in the physical body. Beings who are immersed in this will often run themselves ragged trying to manipulate other people to get with their program. Everything has to be "the best," "the highest," "the most advanced." Often, a difference of opinion or an implication that they don't know something is taken as an attack on their mastery. It is characterized by a nagging dissatisfaction and placing blame: "I have this wonderful vision and if you would just get with my program, I could carry out my Divine Purpose. It's your fault that I'm not living in heaven on Earth." "Your scarcity pictures are blocking Divine Flow. It's your fault that I'm broke." "Why did you create that in your reality? (Please deny what's going on with you, so I can be comfortable. If you were more spiritually advanced, it wouldn't have happened. So, you only have yourself to blame.)"

Spiritual significance and spiritual ambition are strong ego defenses. As Spirit reveals more and more of what you truly are as divine multidimensional masters, the mental and emotional bodies want to embrace it as personal truth by defining and attaching to it. The physical body is usually oblivious to the revelation or simply doesn't buy it. Everyone runs these defenses at some time in seventh, eighth, and ninth levels.

In seventh-level Lightbody, many people fall into a pattern of spiritual manic-depression. One minute they're declaring, "I'm a divine, multidimensional being!" and the next minute they are proclaiming their worthlessness: "I can't do anything right!" They are bouncing between the feelings of multidimensional Oneness and the feelings of separation held in their physicality. The paradox of being so vast and also being in a finite, matter-based body is nothing short of miraculous. Bouncing between the two extremes is an attempt to resolve the paradox. You cannot. Try holding both poles at once. Allow both to be fully present. Toward the end of seventh-level Lightbody, or at least sometime by ninth-level Lightbody, people begin to understand this process and find living in the center of the paradox ecstatic.

You started with following your Spirit. When you're into the seventh level of Lightbody, there is this sense of catching up. You're beginning to operate from Spirit in your everyday life. You find that you step in and out of survival fears. You have days when you're childlike and love everything and get along fine, and other days when "it's the pits" of fear and survival. You're feeling like there are two of you. You will find, as you progress through these stages of Lightbody, that the duality drops out. You find that "you" spend more and more of your time in a state of ecstasy. And you find you can function in that state.

One of the major fears of the mental body through this transition is "If I become a multidimensional being, I will not be able to function on the physical plane." You find you spend more and more of your time being aware of yourself in other dimensions and other bodies on the planet. It's fine. You can still function in that state; it just takes practice.

You begin to activate. Your whole perception begins to shift and in your meditations, you may experience yourself in other dimensions. You may also experience yourself in other bodies on this planet. You may have flashes of being in simultaneous time, where you are so NOW that you are all "NOW"s at once. This is pretty exciting when it happens, because then you become aware of the probabilities and possibilities of everything that you do. You see all those lines of force heading out from you. You become more aware of your connections with other people and of how deep your connection is with Spirit at any given moment.

We have noticed off and on that in the seventh level of Lightbody, the overarching feeling is, "I am going to ascend tomorrow; I'm out of here." You are being hooked up to parts of yourself that are already in Lightbody, parts of your future self. And what this does is it facilitates you to get your act together. You quickly sort through everything in your life and you really find out what's important to you: "Well, I'm out of here anyway, so I might as well do what I want. I might as well have fun; I might as well do what makes my heart sing."

You learn what makes your heart sing, what it is that you really enjoy. When you shift into eighth level of Lightbody, you find that everything that makes your heart sing is directly related to your Divine Purpose on this planet and that you're part of the Plan. In eighth level of Lightbody, you realize "Gee, I'm not out of here tomorrow. I'm here for the long haul." You have a deepening sense of purpose and service. You want to do whatever it takes to assist this planet to Light.

Eighth Level of Lightbody

At the eighth level of Lightbody, the pituitary and the pineal gland, generally about the size of a pea, begin to grow and change shape. As they grow, sometimes you will feel pressure in your head. You may or may not have headaches off and on through this process. If you have a really bad mutational headache, understand that the you on the upper dimensions that is assisting you in this mutation cannot feel your physical pain. So, they first thing you want to do is say, "Yo! I hurt. Can we back it off here?" You have to tell yourself on the fifth and sixth dimensions that it is hurting.

Next say, "Please release endorphins." These are a natural brain opiate that allows the pain to ease off. For some of you, you would rather have little headaches for a month and a half. For others of you, you'd rather have a big headache for 24 hours and get it over with. Find out what works for you, because there are points in this process where your brain literally grows. Your brain gets bigger. You may experience cranial expansion. We have seen people entirely change the shape of their skull, particularly as the pituitary and the pineal open and grow. Also, when your pineal is growing, sometimes it feels like someone has their finger between your eyebrows and they're pushing. You also may feel a pushing feeling at the back of your head as the pituitary is growing.

As you transition into the eighth level of Lightbody, there is an activation of what we call the seed crystals. These three small crystals receive Light languages from the upper dimensions. Two of the crystals are located over your eyebrows, directly over the pupils if you are looking straight ahead. The third one is just below your hairline, in line with your nose.

There is also an activation of the recorder cell receiver crystal (on the right side of the head, about one and a half inches above the ear). In the higher dimensions, there is a structure called a recorder cell crystal. It holds vast amounts of information that the soul has gathered over many incarnational cycles on various planets and stars. Periodically, the recorder cell will download parts of the experiential data into the receiver crystal. When this happens, many people feel a tingling, burning, or liquid sensation in the area of the head where the receiver crystal is located. Suddenly, they have all this information and they can't figure out where it has come from.

The eighth, ninth, and tenth chakras activate. The three to five crystalline templates in the eighth chakra realign, so that your energy bodies change their usual motion into spirals of energy. You begin to hook up into multidimensional mind and begin to receive what we call the "languages of Light."

The pituitary and the pineal function together when they are open, causing what is known as the "Arc of the Covenant." It's a rainbow light that arcs over the top of the head, from the fourth eye to the third eye area. That is one of the decoding mechanisms for higher-dimensional language.

Your brain functioning begins to change and you begin to perceive and think in terms of geometries and tones. This can be a little bit unsettling because you usually don't have a translation available. You may feel that you can't talk to people around you because you have no words for what you're experiencing.

It is very common in the eighth level of Lightbody for people to secretly fear that they have Alzheimer's disease. You may have problems remembering what you ate for breakfast or projecting into the future, and this can become quite severe. The other common thing is that you cannot seem to put a sentence together, or when people are talking to you, it's like they are talking in another language. It's a type of audio dyslexia. The big joke about eighth level of Lightbody is: "To gain the 95% of my brain that I haven't used, why did I have to lose the 5% I already had?" All of the pathways in your brain that you are accustomed to using may become non-accessible while entirely new pathways are being created. You may be getting lots of tones in your ears, bands of light, color, geometry, and motion in your head. You may see flaming Hebrew letters, hieroglyphics, or things that look like equations.

It is a communication from Spirit; it is an encodement. In the early stages, you may have no idea of what's being sent, only that *something* is. When this happens, do the unified chakra technique, unify, and ask for translation facility. You may have to keep asking for quite a while, but that's okay. As you progress through the eighth level of Lightbody, there is a point toward the end, right before you transition to the ninth level, that the translation opens up. All of that stuff that was transmitted from Spirit through this period is suddenly there and accessible on a verbal level.

This is the point of going home. That's the best way we can put it. You are hooking up to your multidimensional mind. The fact that you are a vast multidimensional being is real to you at every level and is undeniable. You become aware of your vastness. Many people bop along through the other stages of Lightbody saying, "Gee, I hope this is real!" It's very wonderful when we see them realize that this process is "real" for them.

Then you become aware that you can be anywhere you want to be, doing anything you want to do. The last vestiges of obligation begin to drop off. Everything you're doing is because Spirit is direct-

ing you to. There is no other reason that you ever need. You'll begin
to operate without a need for reasons and rationales. You are following Spirit with every breath and every step. You say "I'm doing this
because I want to," rather than "I'm doing this because I'm supposed
to, or I ought to, or said I would." You begin to communicate with
people on a whole new level, a level we call "transpersonal." You
interact with someone because your Spirit is guiding you to interact.
You talk because the words are there from your Spirit.

In this stage, people often don't know what to do with you, because your fields have changed. All the tetrahedrons they used to be
able to hook up with aren't in "hook" position anymore. Those people
in your life who want to connect with you through coercion or manipulation or co-dependency drop away pretty fast, because they can't
connect with you anymore. You're no longer operating at that level.
There's a deeper serenity that begins to flow through you and a
heightened, more consistent ecstasy as you remain connected with
your Spirit. You're no longer floating in and out so much; you stay in
the body. You manifest your multidimensionality through your body.

The other thing that happens in eighth-level Lightbody is that
you begin to open up your consciousness, not only through the
dimensions, but also across parallels. You begin to be able to coordinate your energy across multi-realities. At first, this can become quite
disorienting, but, over time, will become exhilarating!

Whatever you say or do is completely guided by Spirit. This
completely shifts the way you relate. It certainly shifts your interper-
sonal relationships pretty fast. It can bring up a whole lot of fear,
fears such as "Will I ever have sex again?" or "Will I ever be able to
hold a job?" Sometimes the answer is a big "no."

The eighth level is one of the most transformative levels. Most of
you are moving very fast and feel at times as though you're going
crazy. You may catch yourself talking in rhyme, unable to talk at all,
or talking backwards. The translation will come as you open to the
new languages and let them affect your fields and cellular structure.
It is literally going into your DNA. Your Spirit is putting through

direct encodements at this point. This is also a mutation of the nervous system. All of your nervous system is sort of being "tweaked up" to handle the new levels of information. You may also find that your eyesight becomes kind of blurry, the ringing in your ears becomes so pronounced you have trouble hearing. The nerves in your ears and eyes, and actually your entire sensory apparatus, are being required to process a lot more information than has ever been processed before. So at times there may be brain scrambles. Be patient with yourself and patient with those around you. Keep your humor around you, because there are days when it's very funny. Another thing that is very common in eighth-level Lightbody is heart palpitations or an arrhythmic heartbeat. This is because the internal, fifth-dimensional circulatory system (called the axial system) is coming on line, and your heart may be receiving dual electrical impulses. This goes on until there is a kick-over point, where the axial system and the autonomic nervous system actually merge their functions, and the heart is basically operating from impulses from the axial system. Eighth-level Lightbody is terribly exciting. When 95% of the Lightworkers were in eighth-level Lightbody, they began to hook up into group mind together, and to bring in entirely new programs in service to this planet. It's like cutting a superhighway to Source for the whole species.

Ninth Level of Lightbody

As you transition into the ninth level of Lightbody, the translation opens and you begin to understand tonal languages. It becomes something you can recognize, instead of it just affecting you. Those geometries and patterns that you're working with in your mind become coherent: they are a language. Some of you may experience "hieroglyphics" or "Morse code" — these are all types of Light languages. They are sixth-dimensional. Your Spirit is using these languages to shift the sixth-dimensional structure of your blueprint into a new template for your fifth-dimensional Lightbody.

You are beginning to embody Divinity. The seventh-dimensional threshold may activate, causing lower back or hip pain, and a feeling of density in the pelvic floor. The seventh-dimensional structures are shifting into alignment with your Oversouls. New Alpha/Omega structures are opening around the physical body, allowing more energy to pour in. The fifth- and sixth-dimensional etheric structures are coordinated through the seventh-dimensional alignment with your Oversouls to receive a new Adam Kadmon Divine Image. You may, at this point, experience body shifts: you may find yourself a whole lot taller, or a whole lot thinner, or bigger, or you may grow wings. You may become aware that you have other body types than that of a human. And you begin to integrate non-human identities into the human identity. This is a vast coordination point for all the levels of what you are.

You are translating the languages of light directly and are aware of yourself at other dimensions, in whatever model you care to use. You are aware of the interconnecting crystalline structure that joins everything.

You become far less connected with caring what anybody thinks about you on a personal level. What matters is how you express Spirit *now* with each breath and with each step you take. Who cares what anybody thinks? They'll wake up: they're doing this, too. Remember, this process is not optional; if you're incarnate, you're mutating.

The pituitary gland is opening further and producing more growth hormone. In some women an estrogen imbalance may occur. You may feel exhausted, depressed, and alienated. Sometimes your periods may become irregular, or you may have changes in your flow.

So, as you began the shift to the ninth level of Lightbody, you began a very powerful shift to your multidimensional self. You are making it real and manifest on this planet now: the master that you are. We see you all as masters; everyone is a master. You came to this planet to master the limitations of separation. Great job, guys! Now the game is shifting into who you really are in your vastness. When we look at you, we know every one of you, at every level of your existence. Do you have any idea at all of how much energy it takes to keep you looking this limited and shielded? An enormous amount.

Well, you no longer have to pretend. All the holds are off. You have full permission and total support to manifest your divinity.

There is usually a massive descension at the beginning of ninth level of Lightbody and a massive one at the end. Now, in the third, sixth and ninth levels, you go into strong re-evaluation. The ninth level can be one of the most difficult because it's at this point that you begin the final surrender to Spirit. You will discover that you do not control anything on a personal level. You will understand that all you have ever been is a divine instrument. You are "Spirit-in-action." Your Spirit determines the income you have, or the income that you don't have; the direction that your work is taking, or whether you work at all. Spirit designs everything: you are a divine instrument. It is the dissolution of the ego-self. This is the final passage through the gate of awakening.

This can be the most ecstatic experience and at the same time it can be the most painful. For most of you, this is what you have worked for, for lifetimes. Yet, when you come up to that gateway, it can be frightening. The ecstasy that exists on the other side of that gate is beyond description in this language. I'm channeling through this body now, but I live in that state all the time. I am never separated from Source: I *am* Source. That is what is offered to each and every one of you, but it does mean surrender at every level of your being. Ninth level is where that surrender occurs, surrender and ecstasy.

Now, on one level, free will is an absolute reality, but from another level, it is a total illusion. This is what our friends at Earth Mission call the "dis-illusionment." It is a vital part of the Lightbody process because it means the final letting go of the "I-self," as you think of it. As we think of it, your mental, emotional, and spiritual bodies are *strictly* tools for Spirit. They do not have consciousness of their own. It is part of the illusion of separation that ego-self has control. This is our viewpoint, and it's okay if you don't agree. Right now, as most of you are in ninth-level Lightbody, Spirit is beginning to push you up against the gate of awakening. You are already experiencing the dissolving of your identities and your context. Allow it. Surrender to it. It is the resistance that hurts.

Follow your Spirit with every breath and every step. Be that vastness here and you'll be exactly where you need to be, with whom you
need to be, doing what you need to do in every NOW-moment. The
survival fears drop out: they become unimportant. As you manifest
who you really are and what you're here to do, all the nagging little
illusions become unimportant and not real. Now, fears may still come
up because you're still living in this world, but you're now able to set
them aside. In the third, sixth, and ninth levels, you're disconnecting
from the consensus reality. You find that when you reconnect, it's
painful.

In levels seven, eight, and nine, you find that you're radiating
light differently than you ever have. Your eyes appear very clear and
different to other people. People will walk up to you and say, "You
look so happy." Remember, many people are in terror over surrendering. Say to them, "I follow my Spirit without hesitation. That is why
I am filled with ecstasy and joy. I suggest you do the same." That is
the easiest thing you can say to them. This will happen.

Some of you may be surrounded by people who are in what we
call the "What if ..." syndrome. "What if the poles shift and we go to
Pluto?" "What if Denver becomes an oceanfront property?" "What
if we're all being controlled by some lizard race that wants to culti-
vate us for a food supply?" All these wild "what if"s will be floating
around you. People will periodically freak out around you. Just stay
centered in your Spirit and you'll know exactly what to say in that
moment.

At the seventh level, people often feel that they're going to ascend
tomorrow: Ashtar is going to come and pick them up in his ship and
they're out of here. This is because the energetic links are being set
up between the you that's in this body and the you that's in your
Lightbody, a you that's a "future self," if you're looking linearly. Because of this, there's a sense of needing to get your life in order. It
works. You say everything you've always wanted to say to other
people. You do all the stuff you have always wanted to do.

By the eighth level, you know that you're staying and a new sense of purpose begins to fill you. You get that you're here and that you're here with something to do, and it becomes a joy. In the eighth level, you quit bopping in and out of your body. We see a lot of Lightworkers tap in multidimensionally, but they don't come all the way into their body. So they flip back and forth. In the eighth level, you come into your body. You will feel more centered than ever, more calm than ever before. You now know that you're not crazy because you're so centered and grounded. You become what has been termed "humanity exalted," as you bring more of your vastness here. By the ninth level, you've brought so much of your vastness here that you've become terribly noticeable.

In the eighth level of Lightbody, your upper chakras are open and functioning. The vestigial spiritual body is now merged with your mental and emotional bodies into a unified field. The eighth chakra's templates are put in order and your fields begin to operate in a different fashion. You hook up with your Oversoul. There's a sense of being connected with Spirit all the time.

As your ninth and tenth chakras open further and you open the eleventh and twelfth chakras, you hook up with the Christ Oversoul and you begin to operate from the Christ level of your being here on the planet. At first, you may step in and out of this and it may feel a little uncomfortable as you go from being Divine Love, Will, and Truth to being a "poor bumbling idiot" again. This soon settles down. Sometime after you go through the Gate of Awakening, you begin to operate from the Christ level all of the time. Some of you have chosen to stay working at the Christ level: that will be your path for here. For some of you, you will begin the hook up to the I AM presence. If you begin to operate from that level of Godhood sometime in the tenth or eleventh level of Lightbody, it will be pretty hard to look human. Pretty hot stuff!

At the ninth level of Lightbody, you're moving into states of being that you have never been in before, experiencing the being state of your own truth, experiencing the being state of your unconditional love, and experiencing the being state of your Light and power.

It is called the Threefold Flame and it exists in the heart of everyone. It is a flame that resonates at all dimensions. Most people are usually strong in one component of it.

At the end of the ninth level, you begin a descension — usually quite massive. You've gone through all the ego surrender and this descension is extremely transformative: you may begin to emit Light.

The last three levels of Lightbody are what we call the "spiritual levels." This is where your fields are completely unified, your chakras are open up to the fourteenth chakra. Your fields are now merged, and you are fully hooked into the Christ Oversoul at every level of your being. You have the hookups to your I AM presence.

Tenth Level of Lightbody

In the tenth level, you begin to manifest avatar abilities. That means that you can be exactly where you want, when you want. Teleportation, apportation, and manifestation come in at this level of Lightbody, because you are fully conscious of being one with the Source and being everything. When you are All That Is, what is not you? You *are* the universe, recreating itself according to your pictures of reality. At the tenth level of Lightbody, you finish the hookups and operate from your vastness, from what we call your Godself. You feel connected with everything. There is not a leaf that falls on this planet that you're not aware of, because you are the planetary consciousness. We want you to understand here that this means that this level of perception is all the way into the deepest part of the human consciousness, all the way into the human genetic consciousness. All of this must be integrated, all the way back to the physical. No one is going to be out flying around the ethers now. You need to bring it all back here.

So, what begins to happen as you hook up with the Oversouls is that those double tetrahedrons have exchanged sides, and you are now operating in a unified field. The geometries begin to move in a double helix. Now in a karma game, you only have two-strand DNA, but in Lightbody you have a three-strand (or more) DNA. So, your body forms a fifth-dimensional strand in the center. You begin to build what we call the "Merkabah vehicle" within your energy structures. "Merkabah" means "chariot" in Hebrew.

The Merkabah is a crystalline Light structure that allows you to pass through space, time, and dimensions, completely in your totality. The Merkabah has a consciousness of its own. You may begin to work with it to travel to other Source-systems. From our perspective, going to Lightbody is only a part of a much larger process. We see all planes and dimensions merging back into the Source for this universe, which then merges with other Source-systems, and so on, back to the One. This is a vast, vast program.

In our viewpoint, there is nothing more beautiful or magnificent than the Divine expressions that you will bring forth on your return. For some of you, that return is to this Source-system. For others, it is a return to a different Source-system and you're here to set up the connections for when they all merge. Some of you are just here to move the planet to Lightbody. Others of you will take over from there, shifting the planet to its next realm, and its next, and its next. We deal with the ascension of whole dimensional systems.

You construct this crystalline Light structure out of your own fields, with the assistance of your Spirit. Now we talk about three different axes with different functions: the Angelic function, the Space Brotherhood or Extraterrestrial function, and the Ascended Master function. These fit together. At the time of ascension, the Space Brotherhood will hook together all the Merkabah vehicles they are building in their own fields, to link around the planet, forming the planetary Lightbody — literally building the vehicle for this planet to ascend. Planet Earth will be taken from the third dimension and the dimension will be collapsed.

The Ascended Master axis will act as directors and navigators. They are here to work with the coordinates for taking this solar system out of this area to a multi-star system. They act as navigators.

Many of the Angelics will go into Lightbody, but others will return to pure energy form. As incarnate Angelics, our energy is the "fuel" for this process.

At the tenth level of Lightbody, you begin to work consciously according to your axis. All of you have all the DNA encodements to do all of these functions. It's just a matter of which part of the process your Spirit wishes you to play with this time.

No one of these axes is "more important" or "better" or "more advanced" than another. Play your part fully.

Eleventh Level of Lightbody

You have built the structure of your Merkabah and you begin to shift into the eleventh level of Lightbody. This is where you decide whether to stay in Lightbody and ascend with the planet, whether you will ascend ahead of the planet and act as advance crew, or whether you will go to pure energy form. This is decided in the eleventh level of Lightbody, when you are hooked up to your upper-dimensional Merkabah vehicle through the axiotonal lines.

The axiotonal lines are part of your embodied Lightbody structure but they also connect you with other star systems and universes. These lines of Light lie along the physical acupuncture meridians and connect to your physical body through something called "spin points." Your Lightbody structure is made up of many lines of Light, intersecting in beautiful geometries. In the course of your mutation, a whole new fifth-dimensional circulatory system was built. Cellular regeneration was accomplished through the axiotonal spin points and you were restructured at the molecular level. Your Spirit has created and strengthened these structures throughout all the levels of Lightbody, preparing your physical body to receive the greater Merkabah.

In the eleventh level of Lightbody, all of these structures are firmly in place and fully activated.

You may have noticed that time is speeding up. It speeds up to the point where it becomes simultaneous. So, you will find yourself kicking in and out of feeling that you're everywhere at once and that you're in simultaneity and then in the time line. You'll get used to stepping back and forth. By the time most of the people on this planet are in the eleventh level of Lightbody, this planet will no longer be in linear time. It will be in simultaneity. You are going to have a lot of fun, because that's when you'll see that "past lives" are a joke: you have lives and they all have resonances.

Every time that you choose Light in any one of the parallels, it affects every single life you have ever had. Ever! That's how powerful it is. One person choosing Light in one lifetime affects the whole planet across time and across all parallels. There are seven to eight million Lightworkers incarnate in this parallel alone. How much effect do you guys think you have? Just what do you think you can do? Anything you want, as long as you follow Spirit.

You are operating fully from your God-self and there is no separation. Remember when, in the lower levels, you were following Spirit for all you were worth? Well, you've caught up! So, you have a few headaches on the way and you get the flu, but now it's the payoff!

What you love to do more than anything in the world is your key to manifesting your part in the Divine Plan. Many of you are here with very special skills and perceptivities to assist the planet. You may be a specialist in intergalactic diplomacy, new family structures, new forms of government, or how to equitably allocate food and other resources on a global scale. Creating new types of community living, new rituals for an awakened spirituality, new Light-based technologies, or new expressions through the arts may be what makes your heart sing.

In the eleventh level of Lightbody, you are manifesting your vision of Heaven on Earth and expressing the ecstasy of your Spirit.

Twelfth Level of Lightbody

At the twelfth level, you act on your decision about what to do. That may be hooking up with other people around the planet or all kinds of things. There are many structures that have to come into place for this planet's final ascension: different councils, new governments, all kinds of things. And you're doing it all right now just by being here. Remember, you are working in simultaneity and you simply become more conscious of it. And you're doing it now. It has already happened, so it *will* happen. A planet ascends from the moment of its creation. Nothing will be lost. The entire planetary history is recorded in the Akashic, so you don't need the memory in your body.

You see, every time you make a choice that isn't in the will of your Spirit, Spirit's choice will always occur, but a parallel reality is spun off to hold the other choice. So, there are quadrillion, quadrillion, zillions of these parallel realities. But as all you guys, sprinkled across the time line, awaken and follow Spirit, all those parallels pull back together. You are now living in a constant merging of all those parallels. So, there's a point when all those parallels have merged, and there's only the path of Spirit from the moment of its creation. There never *was* a karma game except in the records. But not in you: you don't have to carry it with you. You don't carry it in your body, you don't carry it in your mind, you don't carry it in your heart. Pretty exciting stuff! This is how you ascend a planet. You reweave it. Each of those NOW-points is the fabric of what you would call space and time. From our perspective, we see lines of force that come down into each NOW-point, across all the parallels, like "grappling hooks." The dimension gets pulled up across time.

So, as you shift from eleventh to twelfth level Lightbody, this is the final activation of the Divine Plan for planet Earth. This planet goes to Light, shifts out of this dimension and is brought into a multi-star system. Everyone is in Lightbody, and follows their Spirit in total sovereignty and total mastery. Then the whole way back is the expression of the return, at every level of your identity and at every level of your being, as you return and experience your Source.

Questions and Answers

Q. What are some of the other mutational symptoms?

A. There's often a point where food no longer tastes like food to you. You can feel hungry all the time and when you eat, your body doesn't register that it's gotten any nourishment. This is because enough of your Lightbody has become activated that you also need Light as a nutrient. There's an easy trick for this. It sounds crazy, but it works like a charm. Take both hands, palms out towards the sun, and make a triangle with thumbs touching to form the base and your forefingers touching to form the sides and the apex. This acts as an antenna and prism for the Light behind the light. Try this for about fifteen minutes. You will feel your body drink in the Light and then you will feel full.

Also, please eat whatever your body wants you to eat. Throw out the rulebooks. You're here to follow Spirit, not spiritual rules. If you're a vegetarian and your body wants a two-pound steak, please eat it. If you hate sprouts but your body wants them, do it. You may feel very directed to drink alcohol, particularly beer, because it has certain components that your body needs to assist it to mutate. Throw out all the "should"s and "ought to"s around what's OK to eat, because you may find yourself eating some really strange things — like spinach with cinnamon.

You'll find that your sleeping patterns become terribly erratic. You may jump from two hours' sleep a day to twelve, and back again. You may also wake up tired. Remember that you're a vast multi-dimensional being and are working hard in the sleep state. As you open more and more to being aware of yourself in other realms, your physical body gets tired, as though it's doing the work. So, say to yourself "Please tighten up the veil," or "I need a night off."

Remember that you're in control of how fast your Lightbody process moves. The more Light you breathe in, the faster you move this process. Doing the Unified Chakra technique is a very simple basic technique that allows you to build your Lightbody because it allows your chakra system to function as it will in Lightbody and it gently assists your energy bodies to move into a merged state. We suggest that you do this several times a day until you get used to it. Then you can say, "Unify," and you unify in an instant. You will get so that you are naturally in this state. Then when you step out of it, you will find that it feels weird to you. If you find that the outside world is too crazy, simply say, "Unify." If you find that you're picking up too much energy from outside, it's because your chakras and energy bodies are not unified.

The other thing you can do is call forth the energy of Grace in your life. The Divine energy of Grace is the most powerful tool you have on this planet. Grace has enveloped planet Earth and the energy is available any time you need it. Grace Elohim is a very personable being and will talk to you anytime you like. Grace is the Elohim of the silver ray and the energy is visible as sparkly iridescent snow. It looks like fairy dust. So, if you see that around you, you know that Grace is with you.

Grace is the Divine force which allows you to make a complete break with the past in each NOW moment. We urge you sincerely: please do not process your "stuff" or try to "fix" yourself. The universe recreates itself around your pictures of reality, absolutely and impersonally. If you hold a picture of reality that there's something wrong with you or that you need to be fixed, the universe will recreate around this ad nauseam. You'll process stuff from this lifetime, every other lifetime you've ever had, and then you'll start on other planets, and then you'll process the planet itself! Please stop. The force of Grace is on this planet so that this is unnecessary. Please use it; it is your greatest asset.

Use the force of Grace in every aspect of your life. You can Grace your car. If the car's screwing up, call out, "Grace, engine please!" We call Grace the "divine lubricant. " Merlin calls her "Cosmic Crisco." There's a reason for this. Remember those tetrahedrons in your field that get stuck in karmic patterns? If you're locked down with someone and you call on the energy of Grace, this iridescent snow falls down on those tetrahedrons and immediately unlocks them. You can use Grace on everything and Grace is delighted to help you in any way possible — after all, that's her Divine Expression. If you catch yourself processing, please stop and call Grace.

One of the patterns we've seen over and over on this planet is: "If only I could fix 'X' in my life, then I could ascend or go to Light." Well, I've got news for you. As long as you're trying to fix yourself, you're not going anywhere. You are now completely who you are: a vast, multidimensional master in the various stages of Awake and Awakening. There is nothing to fix. It is simply a matter of opening, of awakening, of remembering, and of expressing. So, that's the Ariel lecture. We've been known to beg people to stop doing this. We see so many of you Lightworkers struggling and getting bogged down in everything imaginable. It's totally unnecessary and you don't have time: this planet's moving way too fast for you to process your karma and limitations. Karma is just the illusion of a karma game, and you're leaving that behind.

There is a difference between Gracing something and living in denial. This is not a call to deny different parts of your reality. When you have accessed different parts of the physical body's consciousness or the human genetic consciousness, you are going to have a lot of things (like shame, guilt, fear, and despair) pour out of the body. We need to clear the human genetic consciousness. Processing this will take you forever, because you would process each lifetime separately — each human experience held in the collective human consciousness separately — and you would be constantly dwelling in the past. Grace is always NOW. If you're constantly participating with your Spirit in the NOW and Spirit leads you into the human genetic consciousness, you'll express from the physical body's realities. This is still under the force of Grace; it allows you to just let it go. Express it and move on. Processing keeps you constantly in the past, analyzing and extrapolating into the future. You are never NOW. Call in Grace.

We're talking to you as though the Lightbody process is linear; it is not linear. From our perspective, it is a totally non-linear process. You each have a unique tonal signature, the tone that you are. Lightbody is like a chord. So, if you're sitting at, say, the seventh level, you may have a resonance with, say, your third-level self, so you can be having the flu-like symptoms. You can also have resonance with your ninth-level self, so you begin to hear tonals and see geometries. So, although the Lightbody process has an overall pattern, it is also an experiment that each of you is playing with. You will each do this in your own unique fashion, as you express your divinity. So, we find it pretty exciting and say, "Oh, that's a nice twist. What an interesting thing to put in!"

We strongly feel that transitioning a planet to Light is "high-velocity fun." That's why we do it. We're hoping that soon you will feel that way, too. You've all done this thousands of times before and it's what you do for a good time. Figuring out how you will do it this time is fun. The melody of Lightbody as it plays through you is uniquely yours; that's what makes it so exciting. Every time you take a body type to Light, the experience is completely new. For every planet that goes to Light, exactly what happens depends on the density, the species, and the overall collective consciousness of the planet. The planet doesn't always go to Light, even though its inhabitants may. What makes planet Earth particularly special is that the planet herself is going to Light. That's why there's so much focus on your planet: to assist the planet in this process. That was the promise made to the planetary consciousness when she agreed to be the stage for this karma game.

Right now, there's a major pattern being cleared from the planet, what we call "enemy patterning." In September 1989, the planet released her enemy pattern toward humanity. This means that your planet no longer feels that she must be vindictive to her human population. This heads off many of the foreseen catastrophes on this planet. Even when there are natural disasters — earthquakes, volcanoes, floods — the loss of life will usually be minimal. The destruction of property can be massive, however — a signal to disconnect from that stuff.

There's another thing you can work with. There are points in the Lightbody process where your brain function shifts and you may get headaches. You can ease these by assisting the opening of the pineal and pituitary glands — this is a natural thing that has to happen. In a meditative state, close your eyes and focus your attention right between your eyebrows. It may give you a slight headache and it may take several times, but at some point, you will see a bright flash of light as the pineal kicks over to its new function. For the pituitary, focus your eyes and attention "backwards" into your brain until you see a flash of light. That tells you that your pituitary has kicked over. This will usually ease off the headaches and assist the growth of the pineal and the pituitary glands.

What determines the level of your Lightbody activation is a tonal color sequence. The entire Lightbody process can be expressed in tonal, color, and geometric patterns. You may sense these in meditation, as your Spirit works with your energy bodies. When you listen to toning, some of it will feel good. That's for you. Some of it may not feel good. That's for other people.

Q. Will parallels ascend, too?

A. Free will within a karma game means that you can choose to do something that is not in accordance with the will of your Spirit. Whenever this happens, a parallel reality is spun off which follows what Spirit wanted. This happens every time you make a choice which differs from the choice of Spirit.

As you awaken and begin to follow Spirit, no new parallels are created, and those that were created from your earlier choices are being pulled back and merged. You are living in constant, daily merging of thousands of parallels on this planet. When all these parallels have merged, all you have left is the reality that reflects the path of Spirit from the dawn of creation. There never was, therefore, a karma game.

From our perspective, each NOW-point makes up the fabric of everything, what you call "space and time." From our perspective, we see lines of force entering each NOW-point across all parallels. They are like "grappling hooks" into the third dimension, to be used to pull the dimension "up" into a higher dimension, across time.

You will begin to sense yourself across time and also at this NOW-point in the timeline. By the time most people are at the eleventh level of Lightbody, this plane will no longer be in linear time. You will exist in simultaneity and see the joke about "past lives." All your lives resonate with each other across time and space. When any one of your personalities chooses Light, it affects every other, across all time and parallels. This in turn affects everyone that all these personalities come into contact with. So, just one person choosing to follow Spirit affects the entire history of planet Earth.

There áre seven to eight million Lightworkers in this parallel. Just think what we can all do. Anything! As long as you follow Spirit, there is nothing you cannot do.

Q. How does the planetary process differ from ours?

A. The planet was activated to third-level Lightbody on April 16, 1989. She went into seventh-level in January 1993, entered eighth-level on May 30th, 1994, and entered ninth on October 15, 1994. You can see that the entire Divine Plan is speeding up dramatically. Earth is dumping whole reality pictures. Have you noticed all the recent retrospective programs on TV and in the newspapers: "Let's dig through the Second World War." These historical perspectives have to do with the planet releasing and clearing pictures of reality from the consensus. She is dropping whole packages of experience that have been drummed into her throughout the course of the karma game. The other thing you are going to feel is a sense of incredible impendingness on the planet. There is a constant sense that something is about to happen. Depending on where your orientation is, this can be very stressful or it can seem comforting. "Well, everything is moving along." The polarization is increasing. The planet herself feels like she is going into the classic, spiritual manic-depressive swing. "Oh, I'm turning into a star!" and, "We're going to blow up!"

The planet is requiring that people absolutely drop their enemy patterning. So, all of a sudden, you have a wave of anti-Semitism in Europe. It won't last because there's no enemy patterning to sustain it. It's an expression, more than an action. You'll become aware of how international events have a different feel because they are more of an expression, than an action. Creating a war and sustaining it are actions, whereas expressing hatred is not. Once the hatred is expressed, it usually dies out because there's no underlying etheric blueprint to fuel it. All enemy patterning is being released from the planetary structure and out of everyone. Every "us and them" pattern in everyone's field is up for release.

All kinds of new ideas are coming into the mass consciousness. There are Lightworkers everywhere. How many of you watched *Alien Nation*? It did a lot of prep work. A lot of things are coming into the mass consciousness to allow new ways of thinking, living, and relating. We like the Apple Computer slogan: "Your parents gave you the world; give your children the universe." There's all the work that *Star Trek: The Next Generation* and *Deep Space Nine* have done to teach people about the nature of multiple realities and the nature of time and space as it relates to consciousness. This has been very valuable. They have covered the delicate diplomacy necessary to invite a planet into the galactic community in "First Contact." In "Transfiguration," a being turns into a Lightbody on the helm of the starship Enterprise.

You are going to notice a lot of encodement showing up in music. The "Rave" scene is very powerful. It allows a meeting of people to link consciousness and raise energy for the planet; celebration moves through their bodies. At the same time, there are messages of hate in other types of music. The polarization continues.

The overall feeling on this planet right now is, "What the hell's going on?" So, we ask you to be kind, because as the old pictures drop out, it's scary. The planet herself has a lot of fear coming up.

We ask that you "ground up" rather than down into the planet. The planet is in the middle of a mutation and you grounding into her upsets her. She doesn't need to have to stabilize you right now. She's hard pressed to stabilize herself. In fact, what you can do is to help stabilize her by grounding up into the vastness of your Spirit and then acting as a pole for that energy. This allows the planet to be supported from her own vastness.

Q. What is a "descension"?

A. Descension occurs when a higher aspect of your Spirit comes to reside in your bodies. Now usually you've been channeling this higher aspect first, tapping into a larger part of your vastness. Descensions happen all along this process of mutation. It can be as gentle as a sweet revelatory experience, just being a "bliss ninny" for a few days, or it can be totally disorienting. It may make you question who you are, why you're here, and what you're doing.

A big thing that can happen in a major descension is that your very identity can get blown out the window. The more rigid your ideas about who you are, the more difficult a descension can be. If your systems are more open, it's just "Well, who am I today?" and "The reality for today is ..."

The easier a descension is, the less jarring it is. You have all experienced at least one because it's a natural part of the process. You generally have a descension as you go into levels three, six, and nine, and they vary. Some people think that they're walk-ins, but they're not. A descension can be so dramatic that it looks like a walk-in. We're seeing this happen a lot more because people are having more intense descensions.

Q. Are we affecting the planet's mutation?

A. Of course. Now remember that the universe recreates itself according to your picture of reality. If your picture is that the planet is polluted and being destroyed, then guess what happens: you will have a polluted, destroyed planet. If your picture is that it's a beautiful, self-cleansing planet that sustains its occupants in a most exquisite manner, that's what you'll get. So we ask that you focus on what is beautiful and positive. Running fear about the ozone layer will not help. It'll only make the hole bigger. The hole was designed to be there, anyway, to allow divine forces and rays more access into here.

You can do all kinds of things to help the planet — you can plant trees, you can clean up garbage — without running fear or guilt. Fear can render you immobile. Transform these feelings into a sense of serving the planet. Learn to be a Divine Gardener. Sow a few seeds of Love, tend the new growths of Truth, and reap the manifest fruits of Divine Will.

Q. Was there some angelic event that coincided with the full manifestation of Grace's energy?

A. There have been lots of events. Basically, Grace's energy came around the planet as part of the planetary gridwork in September 1989. Gateways will open up every month from here on in, and you'll get used to it. These are ways for you to access different energies, different technologies, different information and different aspects of your own Spirit. For each one of you and the planet herself, all the hookups are being made to the "you" that's already in Lightbody.

If you don't resist a gateway and let the energy flow through you, it's quite wonderful. If you resist changes, the energy jams in your field. We have noticed here that humans have a real proclivity for living in the future, and they seem to have a liking for event-orientation. One of the problems we've noticed in quite a few groups on the planet is this constant looking forward to the future opening of some gate or another. We would say gates are opening all the time, and it's much more powerful to be NOW and in the present with your Spirit. Those who have been very focused in opening this or that gate at some future point have often missed all the miracles in the NOW moment.

Q. How does the Lightbody process affect animals?

A. A lot of species are choosing to leave the planet right now because the devic consciousness does not wish to retain its particular body type in Lightbody. It wants something different. Now, it's all right to love and care for other species, but remember that all consciousness knows what's going on.

For most species, their bodies are not experiencing mutational symptoms. They are mutating naturally. They don't need to unify their fields like you do because they never split them up. The only species having any trouble is the domestic dog. Cats are fine; their function is actually to help this process. They are excellent channels and the entire feline hive soul has agreed to help humans to ascend, so they are very good to have around. Let them sleep with you if they want to.

Dogs and cats have polarized into holding the poles of the old and new worlds respectively. Dogs are absorbing a lot of the energy being released and cats are bringing in new energies. Dogs seem to be having increased parasite problems, so they need more attention than before. Do the "Invocation to Water" over their food and water bowls.

Q. The axiotonal lines are a natural property of a balanced energy field. By what dynamic do these lines assist in manifestation?

A. It is Spirit that manifests them. You have a hookup into the higher grid systems. Through the spin points, the axiotonal lines in your body hook you up into the crystalline grid systems that exist through every dimension. So, when Spirit wants to manifest instantaneously, those lines light up inter-dimensionally.

In the templates of the eighth chakra, the lines have to line up in exact formation with the crystalline grid. The axiotonal lines hook up through the eighth chakra and go off into different star system grids in both this universe and other Source-system universes. Spirit activates those lines to manifest more of its own vastness through the body, which in turn activates more lines, which allows more Spirit to enter, and so on.

Now, when you get this grid system set up, there's an activation at the eleventh chakra, the gateway to the I AM presence. When the templates are aligned and hooked up to the grids, then you have the manifestation of all god-level abilities. But to do this, you must go through the Christ Oversoul; otherwise you burn your body up.

As you pass through the eighth-level of Lightbody, you have opened to the languages of Light and are beginning to decode them. When you don't understand something, simply open to your Spirit and allow tones to come through your body. This will decode the knowledge held deep within your field. So, just let the tones come through. The sound is coming from the upper dimensions and your body is being used as an instrument. You don't have to do it: Spirit does the work.

Q. What does a high-pitched whistling in the ears mean?

A. It's probably an upper-dimensional being trying to get in touch with you. Go really quiet, say "I am open to receive," and let it come in. You may get tones, words, or melodies.

The Council of Ein Soph has brought in the vow break to speed up mutational clearing. It will remove all etheric crystals. Share it with your friends.

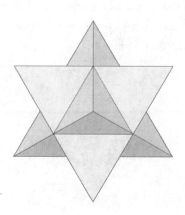

Tools

By the request of many readers of earlier editions of *What is Lightbody*, we have created a Tools section for the 1999 edition. These basic tools and techniques have proven effectiveness in relieving many mutational symptoms, bringing all of your fields into alignment, and living with more peace and joy. The Invocation to the Unified Chakra, The Invocation to Light, and The Invocation to Water have been moved to this section because we consider them basic technologies for ascension.

The Unified Chakra is the base technique of Angelic Outreach. It supports your mutation at every level. The Unified Chakra creates a bubble of Light that allows you to handle vaster and vaster frequencies, and acts like a force field. It helps screen out other peoples' pictures of reality. Most of you walk around running other peoples' energies because your bodies are separated. The main thing for Lightworkers is to get in their bodies and figure out what your energy is.

The Unified Chakra is the best way that we know of to assist you to follow your Spirit with every breath and every step. We suggest that you do the Unified Chakra every single time that you notice that you are in the past of the future. At first that will seem like an incredible task, but if you will do it with discipline, you will find that within two weeks you will unify instantly. By the end of four to five weeks, you won't step out of the merge. Unlike a lot of meditations, you do not leave your body; you stay conscious. It is an altered state, but it is one that you can live in.

INVOCATION TO THE UNIFIED CHAKRA

I breathe in Light
Through the center of my heart,
Opening my heart
Into a beautiful ball of Light,
Allowing myself to expand.

I breathe in Light
Through the center of my heart,
Allowing the Light to expand,
Encompassing my throat chakra
And my solar plexus chakra
In one unified field of Light
Within, through, and around my body.

I breathe in Light
Through the center of my heart,
Allowing the Light to expand,
Encompassing my brow chakra
And my navel chakra
In one unified field of Light
Within, through, and around my body.

I breathe in Light
Through the center of my heart,
Allowing the Light to expand,
Encompassing my crown chakra
And my base chakra
In one unified field of Light
Within, through, and around my body.

I breathe in Light
Through the center of my heart,
Allowing the Light to expand,

Encompassing my Alpha chakra
(Eight inches above my head)
And my Omega chakra
(Eight inches below my spine)
In one unified field of Light
Within, through, and around my body.
I allow the Wave of Metatron
To move between these two points.
I AM a unity of Light.

I breathe in Light
Through the center of my heart,
Allowing the Light to expand,
Encompassing my eighth chakra
(Above my head)
And my upper thighs
In one unified field of Light
Within, through, and around my body.
I allow my emotional body to merge
With my physical body.
I AM a unity of Light.

I breathe in Light
Through the center of my heart,
Allowing the Light to expand,
Encompassing my ninth chakra
(Above my head)
And my lower thighs
In one unified field of Light
Within, through, and around my body.
I allow my mental body to merge
With my physical body.
I AM a unity of Light.
I breathe in Light
Through the center of my heart,
Allowing the Light to expand,

Encompassing my tenth chakra
(Above my head)
And to my knees
In one unified field of Light
Within, through, and around my body.
I allow my spiritual body to merge
With my physical body,
Forming the unified field.
I AM a unity of Light.

I breathe in Light
Through the center of my heart,
Allowing the Light to expand,
Encompassing my eleventh chakra
(Above my head)
And my upper calves
In one unified field of Light
Within, through, and around my body.
I allow the Oversoul to merge
With the unified field.
I AM a unity of Light.

I breathe in Light
Through the center of my heart,
Allowing the Light to expand,
Encompassing my twelfth chakra
(Above my head)
And my lower calves
In one unified field of Light
Within, through, and around my body.
I allow the Christ Oversoul to merge
With the unified field.
I AM a unity of Light.

I breathe in Light
Through the center of my heart,

Allowing the Light to expand,
Encompassing my thirteenth chakra
(Above my head)
And my feet
In one unified field of Light
Within, through, and around my body.
I allow the I AM Oversoul to merge
With the unified field.
I AM a unity of Light.

I breathe in Light
Through the center of my heart,
Allowing the Light to expand,
Encompassing my fourteenth chakra
(Above my head)
And to below my feet
In one unified field of Light
Within, through, and around my body.
I allow the Source's Presence to move
Throughout the unified field.
I AM a unity of Light.

I breathe in Light
Through the center of my heart.
I ask that
The highest level of my Spirit
Radiate forth
From the center of my heart,
Filling this unified field completely.
I radiate forth throughout this day.
I AM a unity of Spirit.

When you finish the Unified Chakra ground multi-dimensionally. Imagine a thick line of Light beginning at the Omega chakra (eight inches below your spine), extending upwards through your spine and on upwards into the upper part of the unified field. Ground into the vastness of your Spirit, not into the planet: she's mutating, too.. Allow your Spirit to stabilize you. Run twelve lines of Light downward from the point of the Omega chakra, opening around your feet like a cone. You are not grounding into the Earth. You're stabilizing yourself across the parallel realities of the planetary hologram.

The *Invocation to Light* assists you to 'lock' the Unified Field into position and increases Light absorption. It is a powerful statement of intent.

INVOCATION TO LIGHT

I live within the Light.
I love within the Light.
I laugh within the Light.
I AM sustained and nourished
By the Light.
I joyously serve the Light.
For I AM the Light.
I AM the Light.
I AM the Light.
I AM. I AM. I AM

LIGHT ABSORPTION TECHNIQUE

As we approach the Eleventh Level of Lightbody mutation, our physical bodies are shifting to be able to metabolize pure Light frequencies as nutrients. This causes our endocrine systems to become unbalanced (especially thyroid, pancreas and adrenals), and many of us have put on weight as our bodies seek the Light that we are beginning to require as part of our diets. As a result, the body will retain fat in the belief that it is starving, and many of us may have had the experience of being hungry and not knowing what we're hungry for, eating many different things in search of that elusive "something" and not being satiated by any physical food that we're eating.

While the physical bodies still require food, adding Light as a supplement to your diet will help stabilize these symptoms. You might also benefit from a full-body endocrine rebalancing as offered by a Lotus Sword surgeon.

First, go outside and face the sun. It is okay if it's overcast—just find the sun in the sky and face it. Palms outward, place your thumbs and index fingers together, creating a triangle shape with your hands. This will create a prismatic tetrahedral structure between your hands. Angle your hands over your heart chakra, and set your intent that your body absorbs "the Light beyond the Light of the Sun." Our sun is a portal that transmits energy from the Orion System, which is our Central Sun, our Galactic Core. When you do this exercise, your body is absorbing Galactic Core frequencies into it, which feeds the Lightbody mutation and makes the body feel full. The prismatic structure you've created between your hands amplifies this frequency. Often, your hands will just pull apart of their own volition when your body has absorbed enough of this energy. You will feel "full" after doing this. Some people feel guided to do this daily, some on a more irregular basis. As in anything else, follow your Spirit as to frequency of this practice.

As far as the physical food that you do eat, it is helpful to add Light to it as well. We do this by reciting the *Invocation to Water* over our food. Like our bodies, our food is about 75% water, so the Invocation will allow us to absorb more pure Light frequency into our body with everything we eat or drink.

INVOCATION TO WATER

I take this, the Water of Life,
I declare it the Water of Light.
As I bring it within my body,
It allows my body to glow.
I take this, the Water of Light,
I declare it the Water of God.
I AM a Master in all that I AM.

Spiritual Hygiene

Whenever you are dropping density of any kind, this technique helps. Do it several times a day if necessary. Visualize the violet flame of transmutation and the silver ray of Grace mixing together to form a beautiful iridescent violet. Then see it pouring into your physical body and filling it. Then bring it through the emotional, mental, and spiritual bodies separately. Also, place sea salt and invoke the rays into your bath water. Wash your clothes and bed-linens with a handful of sea salt, to remove energetic residue. Because you do most of your clearing in your sleep, call in these rays to transmute the old energies as you make your bed. You'll feel so much better. (Universal Detox, Home Sweet Home Enviro-pack)

ENTITY RELEASE

Many times, astral entities will intrude on our fields. Whether conscious or unconscious, we make agreements with them when we have moments of fear or need. These entities will attach themselves to us, usually promising some aspect of ourselves comfort in exchange for living vicariously through us. These exchanges are almost never worth it, as the astral entity is just as subject to distortion and the illusion of polarity as are beings of the 3rd Dimension. They often feed on addictions of various types, be they for substances or people. Some really enjoy anger and violence, and will spur arguments and feed off karmic situations, adding to the intensity of the karma. Sometimes, relationships between people are actually relationships between the entities attached to them! It is always of benefit to release these beings into the Light, so that they can move on to their next stage of development and you can be free of their influence. The Entity Release is a good practice in any "Spiritual Hygiene" program. Some people do the Release on a regular basis, just to be sure no entities have "sneaked" into their fields. *Please be aware, you can only release any agreements that you yourself have with these entities. You cannot release agreements for other people*

ENTITY RELEASE

Call for assistance: "Archangel Michael please bring down the tunnel of Light. Ariel, Azrael and Aru-Kiri, please assist.

"I break any and all agreements or contracts, both conscious and unconscious, that I have made, anyone in my body has made, or anyone in my genetic lineage has made, with any astral entities, thoughtforms, demons, dark forces, elementals, aliens or boogies. Please go into the tunnel, we will take you home."

From the moment you begin an entity release, assume that feelings or thoughts may not be your own. Boredom, spaciness, resistance, „this stuff never works", anger, aches and pains, and grief may all be coming from entities. Identify them and send them on i.e. "entity holding resistance: go into the Light!" Toning is very helpful to ease their release. When you feel clear or lighter, ask Michael to take the tunnel back to the Fifth Dimension.

The Triple Grid

Keeping your space energetically clean is essential — not only because you are transmuting and dropping density, but because everyone on the planet is transmuting also. You are affected by the energies in at least a half-mile radius around you. The triple grid technique is extremely versatile for creating an energetically clean and stable living, working, or driving environment. It's based on the principle of "ask and it shall be given." It's important to be specific in what you ask for.

This technique requests specific groups to do their particular functions. The Legions of Michael are good at infusing energies into a structure and maintaining the structure itself. The Destroyer Force Angels act like a cosmic charcoal filtration system. They create the space for Light to emerge into its next highest level. These beings create Divine potential and expansion of the Light and should not be confused with the Dark Forces, who create condensation of the Light. Circle Security is a branch of the Intergalactic Federation of Planets and Stars. Their job is to set up, keep clear, and maintain interdimensional and inter-universal communication grids.

In the triple grid technique, you ask the specific group to set up their level of the grid, designating the geometric shape, size, and location. Spherical grids are the most stable and easy to maintain, so we suggest working with this geometry for most everyday applications (such as around your home, car, or workplace). You will want to renew the grid weekly or when you notice the energy getting funky.

"Legions of Michael: grid level one, spherical, my house. Destroyer Force Angels: grid level two, spherical, my house. Circle Security: grid level three, spherical, my house."

"Destroyer Force Angels, please spin your grid, spinning out astral entities, stray electromagnetic frequencies, fear, disharmony, anger, adverse astrological influences, expectation, frustration, viruses, fungus, bacteria, worry, astral distortions, miscommunication, sadness, enemy patterning, scarcity, loneliness and spin out anything that hasn't been mentioned in this or any other language, but which you know needs to leave the space at this time." (These are just a few suggestions. Fill in whatever is needed, according to your situation.)

When the clearing feels complete, continue with: "Reverse spin, same stuff." When that feels complete, end with "Stop spin. Thank you."

"Legions of Michael, infuse your grid with the energies of Grace, Faith, Hope, Peace, Purity, Liberty, Harmony, and Victory Elohim. Infuse with love, intimacy, the Unified Chakra, centeredness, clarity, full connection with Spirit, tolerance, clear communication, health, wealth, following Spirit without hesitation, mastery, sovereignty, living Heaven, and anything else I haven't mentioned in this or any other language, but which you know needs to be in the space at this time. Please seal grid. Thank you." (Again, more suggestions. Fill in whatever you need, according to your situation.)

"Circle Security, realign grids to harmonize with upper-dimensional gridworks. Release all distortions and parasites on the grids. Infuse frequencies for clearer communication with Spirit. Seal grid. Thank you."

Grids for your home: We used a possible home grid in the above example. When setting up a home grid, look for what energies in your environment may be adversely affecting you and what energies you need to support you on a daily basis.

Are you in the flight path of your local airport? "Spin out microwave and radar transmissions." Are you fighting with your partner or housemate a lot? "Spin out karmic monads, anger, resentment, miscommunication, referencing the past, obsolete telepathic images, astral entities … ." "Infuse clear communication, compassion, mastery, sovereignty, intimacy, transpersonal positioning, honesty, love … ."

Do you live in an apartment complex with noisy, fighting, impoverished neighbors? "Spin out hatred, violence, astral entities, enemy patterning, scarcity, struggle, hopelessness, stress, other people's karma, inconsideration, fear … ." "Infuse harmony, Divine provision, peace, clarity, gentleness, honor … ."

Are you heavily mutating and clearing? "Spin out density, obsolete pictures of reality, struggle, resistance, fatigue, obsolete genetic encodements … ." "Infuse peace, hope, connection to Spirit, surrender, Grace and Purity Elohim, require of me whatever it takes … ."

Ask the Destroyer forces to spin the grid in both directions continuously. The grid will remain spinning until you ask them to stop. This will help you and you environment to not accumulate what you are releasing.

Grids for your car: Parallel merger disorientation and mutational weirdness seem to be amplified when people are driving their cars. Often, they don't even know where they are or where they are going. Obviously, this can be dangerous. We suggest always gridding your car and to renew the grid every time you leave your home. Many people have found it helpful to hang a quartz crystal from the rear view mirror and to infuse the grids into the crystal. It acts as a reminder to renew the grids. Just put your hand around the crystal and say, "Renew grids." Here are some suggestions on what to ask for:

Place a spherical grid around the car and ask the Destroyer forces to "Spin out spaciness, disorientation, frustration, parallel bleedthrough, adverse astrological influences, other people's karma … ." "Infuse clarity, zen-like serenity, excellent mechanical workings, a stable reality bubble ... ." You can also ask the Legions of Michael to "tractor beam" you to your destination. **Do not infuse invisibility**! People will hit your car.

Grids for your workplace: We want to emphasize that the Triple Grid cannot be used to manipulate other people. It sets an environment where certain energies are more difficult to access and other energies are more easily available. If someone really wants to be a pain, they can; they'll just have to work a little harder. You are setting a space for higher possibilities. In your workplace, "Spin out competition, ego, manipulation of others, self-manipulation, secrecy, enemy patterning, miscommunication, dishonoring, rabid individualism, astral entities, struggle, frustration, dissatisfaction, fear, scarcity, deceit, resentment, obsolete telepathic images, impatience ... ." "Infuse honesty, integrity, vision, fulfillment, mastery, sovereignty, competence, easy co-creation, patience, the Unified Chakra, joy, harmony, humor ... ."

The Triple Grid can be done around a location without you being physically there. Try doing it around the mall, the courthouse, the grocery store, or the post office, before you get there. Perhaps it would be fun to set up and maintain this grid around Congress, the White House, the Pentagon, or the IRS. Remember that it cannot be used to manipulate others; it just makes particular energies more or less easily available.

This is a very versatile technique. We have given you the everyday applications. The spherical geometry is very stable and easy to maintain. Live in it all the time and it will be easier to live Heaven on Earth.

AWAKEN VOW BREAK

I now rescind any and all vows that I have taken to experience the illusion of unconsciousness. As Lightbearer of my genetic lineage, I break these vows for myself and all of my ancestors.

I declare these vows null and void in this incarnation, and all incarnations across time and space, parallel realities, parallel universes, alternate realities, alternate universes, all planetary systems, all Source systems, all dimensions, and the Void.

I ask for the release of all crystals, devices, thoughtforms, emotions, matrices, veils, cellular memory, pictures of reality, genetic limitation, and death. NOW!

Under the Law of Grace and by the Decree of Victory!

By the Decree of Victory! By the Decree of Victory!

As Spirit wills, I ask for Awakening! As Spirit wills, we are Awake!

In the beginning, I AM THAT I AM!

B'resheet, Ehyeh Asher Ehyeh!

"Help! I'm Mutating!": What You Can Do

All techniques and processes in this book are for Spiritual Light Integration. This is not medical advice. If you are experiencing any of the symptoms mentioned, please see your doctor.

A few of these symptoms must be handled by an etheric surgeon, but most you can take care of yourself. By your request, we have added suggestions for which specific Angelic Outreach Potion to use with each symptom. The potion "Magnificence" helps most of them. No matter what kind of mutational symptoms you are experiencing, we suggest that you do four things first:

1) "The Unified Chakra" with the Omega grounding and the "Invocation to Light"

2) Spiritual Hygiene

3) Entity Release

4) The Triple Grid

All of these techniques are in the Tools section. If they have not helped, ask for assistance from your Spirit and your multidimensional friends. You must ask for help or we can't assist you.

Headaches

This is the second most common mutational complaint. We'll break it down by type:

Sharp chronic pain in head, neck, or shoulders: Probably etheric crystals — get them out! Contact an etheric surgeon trained in this technique.

Cranial expansion: If you're getting lumps, bumps, and pressure in your skull, your brain is probably growing. Reach up with your hands and pull the cranial plates apart. This usually does the trick but if not, find someone who does cranial-sacral bodywork.

Pressure between the eyebrows: This one feels like someone has their finger between your eyebrows and is pushing. That's exactly what you do for it. Take your finger and press there for a few moments. Usually, it eases right up. This is the pineal growing. This technique also works for pressure at the upper back of the skull (pituitary growth) and pressure on the top of the skull, center back (the fourth eye).

Severe headache at base of the skull: This is what we call an "under construction" headache. Most people are conditioned to contract their body and energy bodies when they feel severe pain. In this case, if you do that it will increase the pain dramatically. Take your hands and place them over your ears. Now, imagine that as you move your hands away from your body, you are also pushing your energy bodies out and away from your head. It sounds silly, but it often works.

Severe mutational headaches that nothing has helped:

1) Inform the "you" in the fifth or sixth dimension, who is directing this work, that what is being done hurts. The "you" in Lightbody cannot feel your physical pain, so, tell yourself to back it off.

2) Say "Please release endorphins!" These are natural brain opiates. Usually you will feel an immediate release and easing of the pain.

3) Buy some dioptase. This mineral has dark green crystals on a matrix base. We have found it works wonders.

4) Potions good for all mutational headaches: Mystical Articulation and Divine Expression. They boost the mutational headache very quickly and it seems to help a great deal.

Flu-like symptoms: This is the most common complaint because, as you're dropping density, if you don't or can't transmute it, it's got to come out somehow. (Try Magnificence, Subatomic Tonic, and Universal Detox.)

Nausea and Vomiting: Often people who have a lot of stored fear in their bodies get this. Often there is a lot of mucous in your body as you are releasing fear. Say the "Invocation to Water" over your food and drink. If this doesn't help, let yourself vomit. You should feel better quickly. Another thing that may cause nausea is if your energy bodies are spinning too fast. It's like motion sickness. If you put your hands out and tell your fields to slow down, they'll slow. Deliberately slow down your fields. If you are clearing things from the human genetic consciousness in your body, you may have a lot of nausea, and you find yourself vomiting energy. (Use Pathcutter if you are clearing genetics.) This is pretty common. There is also a vent in the sternum that you may get a lot of pressure in. If you think of it as the aperture of a camera, and open it up and kind of spray energy out of your body, it seems to really help. It's the same with the headaches. There is also another one of these vent points at the back of the neck in the middle. If you get a lot of pressure buildup in the head, if you sort of open that up like a camera aperture, it triggers like a fire hydrant and it will often release a lot of pressure in the neck and shoulders.

Diarrhea: We've noticed that people with lots of stored rage tend to get diarrhea. Once again use the "Invocation to Water." You may just have to get used to it, because some people get the runs every time they bring more Light into their bodies.

Muscle Aches and Joint Aches: People with this one usually have lots of stored resistance. This is also very common after a "walk-in" or a strong descension. It can be a rejection reaction at the cellu-lar level. Sometimes it looks like rheumatoid arthritis. Take "Omega 3" fish oil capsules. It seems to lubricate the body. Also imagine that you are lying in an ocean of Light with your head toward the shore. As the waves wash over you, they bring Light into your body. As the waves ebb, they pull out the resistance. (Surrender, Universal Detox, Ecstasy)

Fevers and Sweats: Many folks get this one without the rest of the flu symptoms. Sometimes the fever is very high. Your skin may get quite red. Often, a person's energy bodies are vibrating out of phase with the physical body. You have two ways to approach it:

1) Lower the vibrations of your fields by slowing the spin or imagin-ing them growing heavier.

2) Deliberately try to increase the vibration of your body by trying to make the fever higher. Either way, you should feel a "click" as they go back into phase and the fever should drop immediately. Most people have found making yourself hotter helps. It is easier to do than making yourself cooler.

Tiredness: There are many causes for this. You may be in re-evaluation or working very hard while asleep. In this case, honor the energy drop and rest. Also, if it continues, ask your Spirit for a night off. Notice if your body is doing a lot of releasing. You may need to do a physical de-tox to help your body release density. (Universal Detox, Fire of Purpose)

Other Physical Symptoms

Vibrating while meditating or on awakening: This is a very natural part of the Lightbody process, but is often quite alarming when it starts. It simply means that your vibration is rising. Relax. Enjoy it.

Pain in the exact center of sternum: This is usually the heart chakra opening to a new level. Breathe and call the Silver Ray of Grace into the heart. Then deliberately open your heart chakra. Keep breathing and opening it until the pain subsides. The heart chakra is the multidimensional gateway. It may be like a rusty door and may need the lubrication to open. (Alignment, Ecstasy, Love Potion #9)

Pain in the lower back and hips: If you are in eighth- or ninth-level Lightbody, or you are a walk-in, the pain may be caused by seventh-dimensional Divinity thresholds maxing out. See your etheric surgeon. (E3, Subatomic Tonic, Ecstasy, Heavenly Body)

Arms and hands tingling or falling asleep: This sometimes happens for up to four months. Often this is the laying in of Lightbody structures for etheric healing or surgical abilities. Usually this only occurs in Lightworkers who have this as part of their Divine Purpose. We have also seen a lot of these type of nervous system mutations in eighth-level Lightbody, as the nervous system is being required to handle a lot more Lightbody impulses. If you find your hands or feet going to sleep while you are using them, it is time to do an adjustment in the brain. The pineal gland emits tonal and electromagnetic frequencies that help regulate the electrical pulses in the autonomic nervous system, as well as the pulse of the spinal fluids in all sorts of different rhythms in the body. If for some reason the pulse coming from the pineal gland to the base of the skull into the spine is disrupted in some way, it will cause problems in the nervous system where you may even lose your grip. You may have deep leg jerks as you are trying to go off to sleep. It feels almost like the sheaths of the nerves are trying to be pushed backwards. This can be very uncomfortable. If you put your finger in between your eyebrows, you're pressing on what's called the Ajna center, which is the center which connects to your pineal gland in your brain. Take your other hand and put your finger at the very base of your skull, in the middle. Focus your attention inwards to the center of your brain. What you're going to notice if you are having this nervous system problem is a band of Light, going from the center of the brain to the brain stem, that looks like lightning or like electricity. Start to breathe into it and slow that down until it looks like a laser, bluish-white in color, and about the thickness of a pencil. Once you have got that smoothed out, you begin to pulse the Light. Your Spirit will adjust the pulses to the rhythm that you need, and you will feel your entire body and nervous system relax. Keep this up until you feel fully relaxed. Usually takes a minute or so. (E3, Service One-on-One, Mystical Articulation, Merkabah, Adam Kadmon)

Changes in food habits: You may find you crave some very strange food combinations. Your physical body may need various nutrients in different proportions than ever before. Remember, it's changing at the cellular level. So, throw away your rulebook on diet. Another common experience is feeling hungry or unsatisfied no matter what you eat or in what quantity. Your body is beginning to need Light as a nutrient. First, say the Invocation to Water over everything that you eat or drink. Secondly, do the Light Absorption Technique in the Tools section. (Heavenly Body, Ecstasy, Yod)

Sensory and Perceptual Changes: As you progress in your Lightbody, you go through many changes in how you experience the world. Your senses become more acute and open into the psychic gifts that lie behind them. Also, your multidimensional perception opens up. Here are some common symptoms:

Excessive Sensory Input: Sometimes, one or all of your physical senses suddenly amplify. If this is disturbing, focus on one sense and extend it, gently shutting down all the others. This usually brings the senses back into balance. (Divine Expression, Magnificence, Gifts of the Holy Spirit, Magical Visions)

Ungrounded or spacey: Ground multidimensionally. Also, it's helpful if you focus your attention fully on your feet. Try to feel the texture of what your feet are resting on. This brings you more into your body. (Fire of Purpose, E3)

Low-level anxiety, dizziness, and clumsiness: The brain is opening in its perceptions across multi-parallels. The body is beginning to sense that perhaps it could exist in more than one reality at a time. If you find that focusing on your feet isn't working, run a grounding cord from your Omega chakra, eight inches below your spine, up your spine, up into the upper chakras, grounding into your vastness, into Spirit. Run twelve lines of Light downward from the point of the Omega chakra, opening around your feet like a cone. You're not grounding into the Earth. You're stabilizing yourself across the parallel realities of the planetary hologram. To your physical body, opening perception across parallels is like being in a reality earthquake. Put yourself in a doorway and hold on to the door jambs. Your body's instinctive response will usually calm right down. This usually seems to help, even in the worst cases. (Serenity, Mastery, Planetary Service, Divine Mother, Divine Expression)

Objects appear to move, melt, or shimmer: This is a common perception as you move into multidimensional sight. You may be beginning to sense the atomic motion within everything, parallel realities, energy flows in the room, or the beginning of "far-seeing" clairvoyance. If this is unsettling to you, remember that your physical body exists "NOW," in this parallel of third-dimensional reality, and you can use it to re-center your consciousness. Simply extend any physical sense, except your sight, and your body will bring you fully back into your usual reality. Also, focusing on your feet, as in the previous paragraph, helps greatly. (Mystical Articulation, Sub-atomic Tonic, Magical Visions, Gifts of the Holy Spirit, Love Potion #9)

Hazy Vision: If you open your eyes after a deep meditation, sometimes the room appears hazy. We have seen people virtually blinded. This means that you are between physical sight and clairvoyant or multidimensional sight. Your vision is neither here nor there. To adjust it, try yawning. Yawning is one way that people shift their bodies and consciousness through different energy frequencies. You can consciously use yawning to shift levels of perceptivity. Close your eyes and yawn, with the intent to make your vision third-dimensional and bring it back here. Or close your eyes and yawn with the intent to shift your sight into other psychic or dimensional levels. Your optic nerve is being required to handle a lot of impulses that it has never had before. Blurry vision is very common, especially in eighth-level Lightbody. If you find that you can't find any comfortable distance where your eyes will focus, we suggest that you **not** go out and get eyeglasses. Generally, within a weeks' time, you won't be able to see again. Your physical sight is very linked to the perceptions of the mental body. As new perceptions are coming in through your brain and through the spiritual body, it's very natural that some of the physical sight turns off as the mental body becomes less predominant. It will come back. It may take a few months, but it will usually come back. (Mystical Articulation, Subatomic Tonic, Magical Visions, Love Potion #9)

Audio Dyslexia: Very common in eighth-level Lightbody. When you listen to someone speak and you can hear the words, but your brain can't seem to make sense of them, it is called "audio dyslexia." Your brain functioning is becoming non-linear. The translation faculty from non-linear thought to linear language may not be on line yet. There are levels of Lightbody where it briefly seems like some people are talking in a foreign language, but you know they are not. This can be scary, because the mental body may send out panic signals and fears about going crazy. You are becoming very sensitive to people's energy. On this planet, what most people say verbally is totally at odds with what they say energetically. Most people don't know that they are lying or not being genuine. You are becoming so sensitive to someone's energy that you can no longer decode their verbal lies. The audio dyslexia is a brief stage while building Universal Mind translation facility and the ability to sense truth in yourself or others. Take a breath, laugh, and wait for further instructions. (Mystical Articulation, Transpersonal Transformation)

Hearing beeps, tones, music, or electronic "Morse code": It may be tinnitus or it may be a Higher Light transmission. We suggest that you relax and simply let the signal come through. Don't worry about understanding it; the translation facility comes over time. (Mystical Articulation, Surrender, Yod, Gifts of the Holy Spirit)

Memory Loss: This is a natural part of Lightbody. As you begin to live more and more in the "NOW," you lose the ability to reference to the past. This could be an inability to recall karmic patterning and relationships or simply to remember what you had for breakfast. There are many people living with the secret fear that maybe they're in the beginning stages of Alzheimer's disease. A very few may actually have the disease but the vast majority are simply living more

"NOW." This break with referencing to the past can be very freeing. Clutching the past fosters the fear of change. You realize how much of your energy is tied up with preserving the past, reminiscing, chewing over "what might have been," or holding on to the way it's always been. Some people are also finding it very hard to project into the future. This, too may be unsettling, because you may miss appointments and such. The old world couldn't function without dwelling in the past, projecting into the future, and living by a clock, if not a stopwatch. In the new world that is emerging, people will live by their Spirit, delighting in the "NOW." As you become fully NOW, you literally become "in the world, not *of* the world." You live in a separate world from other beings. (Alignment, Mystical Articulation, Surrender, Angelic Outreach Alpha Omega, Paradigm Shift, Yod)

Spiritual significance, spiritual ambition, spiritual manic-depression: Just about everyone goes through these at some time in their Lightbody process, usually at the seventh, eighth, and ninth levels. They manifest from trying to deny or run away from guilt, shame, survival patterns, and feelings of separation held in the physical body. Spiritual significance and spiritual ambition are ego defenses and, unfortunately, the person rarely knows (or admits) that they're running them. (Mastery, Transpersonal Transformation, Alignment, Planetary Service, Quantum Wealth, Surrender, Magical Visions, Divine Mother, Love Potion #9)

Blowing lightbulbs and fuzzing electronics: At many points in the Lightbody process, you may find that you are buying an awful lot of lightbulbs. You'll notice that they tend to burn out or flicker when you are next to them. Your television may ghost or snow when you walk by or are merely in the room with it. Your speakers may "static" when you are near them. These little annoyances are caused by changes in your electromagnetic body, your auric field. There are several times in the Lightbody process when the electromagnetic body stretches. Sorry, there's nothing you can do for this one that we know about, except try to align your energy with your objects. With the electronic object off, try to merge your energy fields with the object. It is very normal to have some problems with electromagnetic frequencies. You may be much more sensitive to them than you have been before. You may feel radar. You may feel the electromagnetic waves. You may feel things coming off your television. Try the technique of merging your energy with it. (E-3, Subatomic Tonic, Adam Kadmon, Yod).

THE ANGELIC OUTREACH POTIONS

Many times we've heard Lightworkers exclaim "I wish you could put that energy/entity/quality/ability in a bottle!" So we did. We listened to your requests, looked at the planetary energies impacting you now and in the recent future,* and created these "potions" to be of assistance.

In the past, these potions have included gem, flower, rare gas, and starlight elixirs and essences, in specific proportions. We infused each potion with its appropriate higher-dimensional qualities. The main purpose of these ingredients was to ground and buffer the higher frequencies for the physical body.

On May 30th, 1994, a dramatic shift occurred in the Divine Plan for planet Earth. The timetable for ascension was moved up and, due to this change, we feel it is appropriate to take the potions into pure frequency. We will no longer use the essences and elixirs to create a bridge and soften the energies. Your bodies are now prepared to absorb the higher-dimensional frequencies directly.

All of our potions are infused by various members of the Council of Ein Soph. They are designed to be pure frequency/energy infusions. The Council infuses the potions into a distilled water base through intensely powerful tonals and "locks" the frequencies into water held in "mother jars". The Council protects these frequencies and maintains their purity both in the mother jars and in the individual potion bottles. The Council is aware of every bottle of these potions no matter where they may be on the planet. Periodically, the council chooses to "upgrade" the frequency of some of these potions. When this occurs, the frequency is upgraded in every existing bottle of the potion, so you can be assured that no matter how long you've owned a given potion, it is always maintained at optimal potency.

The potions are usually taken internally, in a quantity directed by Spirit, though some folks have come up with some very creative uses for their potions! (Such as: eyedrops, douches, in bathwater, or in aromatherapy diffusers and table fountains.) All potions come in one-ounce dropper bottles.

Use of these products, whether internally or externally, allows your body to easily absorb and align with the frequencies they carry. They have been created by the Council in service to the ascension of planet Earth and in support of the mutation of Earth's inhabitants into Lightbody.

— Of the Source in service to the Source,
Ariel Elohim for the Council of Ein Soph ("the Crew")

*"recent future" is a phrase Ariel uses to express non-linear time

All of the potions described here are for spiritual use only.
These are not medicines and no medical use is suggested.

ANGELIC OUTREACH POTIONS

ADAM KADMON

Allows the integration of the Adam Kadmon blueprint into the Physical Body helping to recalibrate the endocrine system, the nervous system, the circulatory system and the magnetic bodies to Universal pulses and frequency as well as the pulse and frequency of Planet Earth. Adam Kadmon gently aligns the body's etheric blueprint to entrain to the Divine Blueprint thereby supporting all the bodies' transfiguration to Light. This is a good one to use just before bodywork of any kind and especially Lotus Sword Integrative Services. Helps to bring latent Divine Structures in the bodies into manifestation. Nice complement to Merkabah work as well. Infused by Merlin, Uriel, Aru Kiri, the Devic Kingdom, as well as, Ze'Ertu, Ze'Ama, and Ze'Erzah of the Ze'Or Continuum.

ALIGNMENT

Alignment to your Spirit is essential for weathering the coming changes. This potion is for aligning every part of you to the One Probability, Spirit, the Earth and Humanity. Polaria, Victory and Harmony Elohim add their energy to this one.

ANGELIC OUTREACH/ALPHA OMEGA

Holographic access formula. Allows you to access the command codings for holographic restructure. Assists with shifting patterns/ structures on a holographic/planetary scale. Assists in creating synthesis of 3rd, 4th and 5th Dimensional programs. Assists in manifesting Heaven on Earth. This potion is infused by the Ein Soph, the Collective Voice of Humanity, the Shekhina, and Gaia.

CO-CREATION

Co-creation is a more refined version of the „Group Synergy" potion. It still carries the energy of evolutionary group synergy; however, the new potion is a higher frequency and also smoothes out frictions while working with others. Allows the bodies to orient to mutually beneficial, transpersonal positions for maximum productivity and high-velocity fun. Assists with the co-creation of Heaven on Earth. The Christ Consciousness infuses this one.

DIVINE EXPRESSION

This potion assists in opening all parts of yourself to the creativity and expression of Spirit, especially toning. Some folks have found it very helpful for easing all kinds of anxiety and fear. Also great for connecting to the Cosmic Joke. Coronis in a bottle.

DIVINE MOTHER

Helps access the female frequencies of divinity. Allows nurturance of the body. Carries the energies of comfort, compassion and nurturing. Helps with feelings of „Cosmic homesickness". Very sweet and gentle. This potion is infused by representatives of the Office of Divine Mother: Isis, Mother Mary, Quan Yin, Krizani and TaMa.

ECSTACY

Opens the capacities of all of the bodies to Divine Ecstasy. It assists the 5th, 6th and 7th-Dimensional structures to fully interface, trinitizes all polarities, and helps the Kundalini to awaken. Several folks infuse this potion: Isis, Osiris, Polaria, and Grace and Rapture Elohim.

ESSENTIAL EVOLUTIONARY ENCODEMENTS (E-3)

This potion assists in the integration of multi-species, multi-Universal encodements in the DNA. These genetic encodements have already been activated and the multi-universal orientations are beginning to open and manifest. E-3 assists you to integrate extra-terrestrial perceptivities and orientations into your humanness (and on a vaster scale into the hologram for life on planet Earth). It allows your mental body to follow Spirit with ease, open its closed systems and integrate a vaster sense of identity. It fosters a sense of interconnectedness within the universe and an awareness of yourself in other species on other ascending planets within and without the Love-universe. This allows you to cognate what is essentially „you" beyond the human cultural context. It softens human-centrism and xenophobia, allowing you to access new brain functions and non-human perceptivities and skills. You become a coordination point for the ascension across multiple universal systems, multiple planets, multiple species types, and truly manifest your essential nature through your human form. The various essential genetic encodements of many different species are infused by the entire Council of Ein Soph.

EXULTATION

This potion assists you to manifest the divine perception, abilities and childlike wonder that characterize tenth level Lightbody. Because of the synthesis between the positioning teams and the transition teams in 1995, the transition teams have not been exhibiting true tenth level Lightbody manifestation. Now that the positioning teams are in ninth level Lightbody, it is extremely important that this manifestation begin. This potion carries frequencies to soften over-sensitivity to collective transformational shock and trauma, as well as resonance to ninth level Lightbody. Infused with the Flames of Love as Sanctifier and Redeemer, Yod Spectrum, and Adam Kadmon blueprints, as well as, Ze'Or electro-magnetic recalibrations, it assists you to embody Divinity, integrating divine perception and abilities all the way into the cells. This potion is infused by the Offices of the Meshiakh (Christ), Shekhina (Divine Mother), and YHVH (Divine Father), Ze'Or and Takh Continuums.

FIRE OF PURPOSE

For accessing and manifesting your piece of the Divine Plan with clarity, focus, and Joy. This potion is very helpful for those people who are having trouble with mutational fatigue. Aru Kiri in a bottle.

GIFTS OF THE HOLY SPIRIT

Prepares the bodies for reception of the gifts of the Holy Spirit. Assists in accessing the Christ level of the Oversoul and manifesting it here. Acts as a bridging frequency into the I AM. Exquisite! Infused by the Holy Spirit Shekhina.

HEAVENLY BODY

Designed to help you bring your vision of your perfect body into physicality. Heavenly Body is helpful for anyone who wants to recreate their body in a greater state of health, change their body type or weight, bring new motions, skills or grace into their body. Heavenly Body will rapidly orient you to what exactly is keeping your body in any given shape or movement and help you manifest thought into form. Great for dancers, martial artists, shapeshifters, athletes, etc. Infused by Ze'Ertu, Ze'Ama, and Ze'Erzah of the Ze'Or Continuum.

LOVE POTION # 9

Assists in opening the heart chakra into deeper and deeper levels. Helps dissolve heart chakra armoring thereby relieving much chest and upper back pain. Expands capacities for experiencing and expressing unconditional love. Infused by Michaelilu Elohim, Rapture Elohim and the collective Golden Angels. Use liberally.

MAGICAL VISIONS

Opens the sight and vision of the Magical Child. Assists you to quickly parallax your „reality" into a perspective of magic, miracles and play. Opens you to experience the beauty and wonder in the High Astral Plane. The Fairy and Elfin Kingdoms are assisting our ascension into the 4th Dimension, therefore, representatives have helped to infuse this potion: Arianna, Pan, Lightning Bolt, Skorm, El Veron, The Merlin, and Hope Elohim.

MAGNIFICENCE

For integration of new frequencies into all of the bodies. This potion eases all mutational and descension symptoms and allows the body to delight in becoming Light. Try this potion along with the Unified Chakra *first*, before any other remedy. Often this is what you need. Quan Yin and Polaria zap this one.

MASTERY

This is for manifesting 5th-Dimensional identity and vision. Living as the Masters we are all the time and co-creating Heaven on Earth is what it's all about. Very helpful for accessing and writing out your multi-dimensional vision. Ariel Elohim and Ascended Master Serapis infuse this one.

MERKABAH

Opens, balances and evens out the spins of all Merkabah geometries. Helps you understand the Merkabah functions. Aids focus and pranic breathing. Assists in fully conscious contact with Spirit. Contains the advanced Unified Chakra with all spin, speed and unification co-ordinates. This one is infused by: Melchizedek, Michael, Uriel, and Metatron.

MYSTICAL ARTICULATION

Bio-transducer booster for accessing and translating Languages of Light. Opens up the conscious mind into multi-dimensional perceptions. Particularly good for people who can't remember or don't get much when they meditate. Also great for relieving mutational headaches, forgetfulness, and the effects of having low endorphin production. Helpful for all eighth level Lightbody type symptoms. Merlin and Metatron formula.

PARADIGM SHIFT

Assists with personal integration of holographic changes. Allows integration at all body levels including the physical. Helps with the interface of inner reality with outer reality. Personal manifestation formula. Helps you recognize and alleviate symptoms of: denial, delusion, spiritual authority, spiritual significance and spiritual ambition. Refocuses the change from mental concept to feeling and embodiment. Infused by the Shekhina Presence, Christ Consciousness and the Takh Continuum.

PATHCUTTER

This is a cellular release formula. It eases the expression and release of emotions, density, survival patterning, and karma matrices held in and around the physical body. It removes the resistance to feeling the deeper truth. Use very sparingly and under the direction of Spirit. Intense, but it helps a lot. Purity Elohim and Aru Kiri infuse this potion.

PLANETARY SERVICE

This potion is created for people whose design is to work with the planet, planetary grids, landmasses or anything vast. It specifically helps to stop your Lightbody wiring from frying or power surging. It assists you to smoothly bring energies and multi-dimensional perceptions all the way into the physical body for more effective Lightwork. As it assists your ability to shift consciousness, it also contains elements to soften spiritual significance, cut spiritual ambition and maintain compassion for others. Eases cognitive dissonance between 5th-Dimensional and above orientations and 3rd-Dimensional manifestations. Merlin, The Devic Kingdom, Aru Kiri and Uriel infuse this potion.

QUANTUM WEALTH

Also known as IMF, or Interdimensional Monetary Flow. This formula is designed to help integrate at all levels that Spirit is the provider of all resources. Aids you to surrender into quantum wealth. Yeah! This potion has a synergy of Victory and Faith Elohim, S'eorlah Takh, and Arianna.

SERENITY

This potion is created under the auspices of Faith, Peace and Victory Elohim. It is designed to help you stay centered and calm in the midst of any type of extreme change, be it personal, mutational or planetary. It eases transformational shock and trauma. Serenity cuts through fear and the tendency to focus on negative or destructive possibilities. It assists you in seeing the perfection of the Divine plan in all things, and living Heaven on Earth as your Spirit is creating it around you.

SERVICE ONE-ON-ONE

Designed for people who do one-on-one work. This potion acts like a tonic for the body's wiring: keeps the axiotonals open and flowing smoothly for doing hands-on work. It keeps your body balanced with whatever frequencies are coming through in service to your client, and it has elements designed to assist you in being able to empathize and perceive clearly without taking on your client's energy. It strengthens diagnostic and counseling abilities. It contains frequencies to ease karmic monads (healer/healed, enabler/enabled, savior/saved, guru/disciple). It helps you interact with your clients transpersonally and maintain a 5th-Dimensional perspective. Infused by Raphael, Quan Yin and Adama Rex.

SUBATOMIC TONIC

This one is for molecular integration of a new octave of Spirit. Tashira asked for this potion to assist in the awakening and integration of teleportation, aportation and translocation as well as the manifestation of the Gifts of the Holy Spirit. Makes your particles tingle. This potion is infused by the Holy Spirit Shekhina.

SURRENDER

This potion assists you to go through the Gate of Awakening by surrendering to your Spirit. It helps to collapse closed systems, ego defense structures, denial, and resistance. Provides great assistance in being a clear channel for higher dimensional frequencies and beings. The entire Council of Ein Soph infuses this one.

TRANSCENDENCE

This potion is designed to soften the discomfort of ninth level Lightbody. Its frequencies ease alienation and resistance to „the Dis-Illusionment" by assisting you to stay in the Now, with your heart open and all your intent fiercely directed towards your Spirit. This potion contains holographic access coding designed to recalibrate the brain gland pulses, correct your hormone balance and boost your immune system. It is also infused with the Flames of Love as Requirer and Purifier. Hang in there! The process you are in is holy. When it is complete, you will be filled with gratitude. This potion is infused by Hope, Faith, Grace, Purity, Liberty, Peace, Rapture and Victory Elohim: and the Takh Continuum.

TRANSPERSONAL TRANSFORMATION

This elixir assists the physical, emotional, and mental bodies to shift from personal to transpersonal relationships. It is especially helpful when dealing with lovers and relatives. Grace Elohim and El Veron infuse their energies.

UNIVERSAL DETOX

Designed under the auspices of Grace and Purity Elohim, with assistance from the Ze'Or. It allows the bodies to let go of resistance to change, cuts addiction, brings up vitality, helps you feel nurtured, balances yin/yang, promotes change without denial, and fosters a new vision of health. It clears toxins to the spiritual, mental, and emotional bodies such as: destructive thoughts and emotions, E.L.F. waves, microwaves, boogies, cords, vows, past decisions about health, process addiction, 4-D distortions, and other people's pictures. It clears toxic residues from the etheric blueprints. Universal Detox should be used very sparingly, and may be used in conjunction with a good physical detoxification program.

YOD

Allows the bodies to receive and absorb the ten YOD superscripts essential for smooth mutation. Essential nutrient for Lightbody. The Takh Continuum and Ariel infuse this potion.

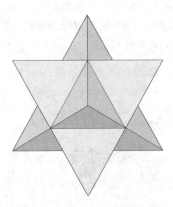

ANGELIC OUTREACH POTION SETS

HOME SWEET HOME ENVIRO-PACK (Two Potion Set)

Everybody needs an energetically clean, secure and supportive home. The Enviro-pack is created in two parts. The first part, „Cleanse" is designed to clear out old thought-forms, emotions, astral residue, boogies and old energy. The second part, „Seal", seals the space after you've cleansed it, and is designed to maintain your environment as a supportive haven for who you are as a Master. It will help you maintain harmony and unity among your bodies and clear communication with Spirit. The Enviro-pack comes with instructions. It is infused by Purity and Rapture Elohim and Uriel.

SURF'S UP!

This new set is designed to assist you to handle the extreme holographic shifts that we are experiencing. The potions act on your perceptions of the outer holographic realities and the oils affect your inner reality landscape. You are likely to need all four of them at some point in the next few months; so, they will not be sold separately. We all must learn to surf these energies and this set will help you ride the big tsunamis more Gracefully.

ALCHEMY OIL: *Reveals the Mystery of Divine Creation.* This oil assists you to open the myriad of potentials within you, selects the highest ones and births them into manifestation. Opens your inner realities into ever-expanding capacity for the highest potentials to be manifest.

SOVEREIGNTY OIL: *Reveals the Mystery of Divine Uniqueness.* No two beings ever see 'reality' the same. This is the gift of Divine

Uniqueness. This oil stabilizes your inner reality landscape. Assists you to take a stand for what you choose to participate with as real.

DESTINY POTION: *I want it All, I want it Now, and I want it Delivered!* This potion allows you to use the collapse of linear time to best advantage- to manifest Heaven on Earth more quickly. When all the energies seem to be 'stuck' or everything feels impending, this potion acts like a holographic fast forward button. Destiny opens your outer holographic reality into ever-expanding capacity for rapid manifestation of the highest probabilities. Infused by Ariel, Michael, Raphael, Razael and Tzadikiel in their Elohim Creator Source functions.

ARREST POTION: *A random realities emergency stabilizer tonic.* Many people are feeling like they are 'walking in a dream' or 'tap dancing on reality quicksand'. This potion stabilizes your perceptions of the outer holographic reality so you can get your bearings. It acts like a holographic pause button, slowing down the outer stimulus. It also puts your impact on the hologram on pause. This can be very helpful when you are having "one of those days" and you don't want what you are focused on to manifest in your reality. Infused by the Ze'Or, the Takh Continuum, Coronis, Liberty and Harmony Elohim.

Do not take DESTINY and ARREST together! They have somewhat opposite effects. The oils can be used together or with either potion. All Mysterium Oils are infused by the Office of the Divine Father through J.J. Wilson. All Angelic Outreach Potions are infused by the members of the Council of Ein Soph through Tashira Tachi-ren.

THESE POTIONS AND OILS ARE SOLD ONLY AS A SET.

BASIC USAGES

1) Seven drops under the tongue three times a day, or as directed by Spirit.

2) Place a few drops onto the crown chakra (or any other chakra) and rub it in.

We have found this to be a particularly good method of bringing the vibrational effects into the body.

3) Place a few drops in your favorite beverage!

4) Use in your environment.

   a. Walk the perimeter of a room releasing drops every few feet.

   b. Place drops in the corners of a room.

   c. Place drops in water (preferably distilled water) and use as a mist in an atomizer, spray bottle or even your humidifier. You can mist your plants, animals or your own body.

   d. Place a few drops on a bell, gong or chime and then ring the bell to resonate the vibration throughout the room.

   e. Place drops on any kind of amplification grid.

5) Use with your animals.

Our pets are mutating too. They don't have the same mental screening mechanisms that we do. Therefore they see and sense parallel realities, astral entities, energy shifts and can become frightened, aggressive, sick, or disoriented. We have found that if our animals are frightened or disoriented a few drops of Divine Expression in their drinking water really helps. If they are processing for you, or you need to move your home, a little Pathcutter in their water does wonders. If they are aggressive, squabbling, or you need to introduce a new animal to your home use Transpersonal Transformation and Co-Creation in their water. Try Serenity in any case or in combination with any other potion. If they are mutating, Magnificence will clear up the symptoms. If your pet is in ill health, Heavenly Body combined with clear visualization of sparkling health will assist them. Universal Detox has been used as eye drops, ear drops, and in pet's water to clear parasites, fungus, and infection with good effect.

SPECIFIC USES BY POTION

HEAVENLY BODY:

Add a couple drops to your shampoo, liquid cleansers, astringents, body lotions or bath.

Caution: Heavenly Body is a manifestation potion – it will give you more of what you focus on and make "REAL". So, be aware of what you are making "REAL" about your physical body when you are taking this.

For athletes, martial artists etc.: place a few drops on your equipment at the points of physical contact (e.g. the grip of a tennis racquet). The equipment or instrument will show you its natural movement. This enables you to feel comfortable learning a new skill or honing an ability. It will all feel somehow familiar and you will naturally attune to the perfect motion.

For those changing their diet for health, appearance or experimentation, one drop of Heavenly Body on your food or in a drink will help you discern the effects on your body of what you are ingesting, so that you can either change what you eat or change its effect on your body. When taking supplements with water, place one drop in your water for the same effect.

MAGNIFICENCE:

If you are in a descension, try rubbing it onto your feet. It will help the energy to come all the way into your body. Massage into aching joints. For all-over mutational discomfort, place a few drops in bath water and soak your cares away!

PATHCUTTER:

Pathcutter should only be used when you are already releasing and cutting a pathway through the human genetic consciousness. Otherwise, it will throw you into processing from your physical body. We have found that if a part of your physical body is holding onto an energy, Pathcutter applied directly to that area and rubbed into the skin helps the body let go of the energy. We've also found Pathcutter to be helpful just before a Karmic Matrix Removal and for two weeks afterward. Pathcutter breaks your resistance to releasing or expressing an energy. It takes you to the state of „Spirit, require of me - whatever it takes!"

QUANTUM WEALTH:

Place a few drops on your checkbook, wallet, pockets, purse, etc. Definitely a good one to place in your environment as well as your body. It is capable of allowing you to open to Universal Flow in ways you have not thought possible. One of the first things Quantum Wealth may do is show you places where you are blocking flow or seeing lack in your life. Just see this as information and don't make it "REAL". Allow Quantum Wealth to remove the blocks and continue to focus on the abundance you have in your life.

SERVICE ONE-ON-ONE:

For those practitioners who wash their hands between clients, a drop of this potion on each hand is a nice way to shift your energy. A few drops in your beverage while working with clients helps keep all your wiring and channels open and helps keep you transpersonal.

UNIVERSAL DETOX:

Use sparingly! Follow your Spirit!

HOME SWEET HOME ENVIRO-PACK:

The Home Sweet Home Enviropack is for energetically cleaning your home, office or any space that may be a bit stale, dreary, depressing or even downright creepy. You can adjust the strength of solution to address the intensity of the energy present.

You can use Cleanse and Seal anytime. They can be taken internally – use Cleanse first followed by Seal. Great used with the Entity Release and Grid Techniques. Cleanse is designed to clear out old thought-forms, emotions, astral residue, boogies and generally old energy. Using Cleanse and Seal will help maintain harmony and unity among your bodies and clear communication with Spirit.

Or you can spray your environment. Just keep two bottles on hand – one for Cleanse and one for Seal. Use 2-7 drops in each bottle with distilled water and spray the area – first with Cleanse and then with Seal.

Spray your whole house with Cleanse first. In particular spray all doors and windows, mirrors, the ceiling, floor, corners and don't forget the closets! If you adjust your spray bottle to "stream" you can incorporate sacred symbols into the process by drawing symbols onto the ceiling, floor, mirrors, windows, balconies, etc. As you walk around the space use the Entity Release.

Now spray all the same places with Seal. This time grid and invoke whatever energies you want into the grids. We suggest the

Elohim of Peace, Grace, Purity, Faith, Hope, Victory and Harmony as well as Elohim of the colored Rays you resonate with.

These are basic instructions. This process can be done as high magic ritual or just light maintenance depending upon your focus, intent and the elements you include in the process. Be creative and use strong intent.

You can set specific grid energies for your space. Just remember what energies you've set up because they **will** affect people. If others feel uncomfortable in your space, you may need to adjust the grids you've set up.

All of the potions described here are for spiritual use only. These are not medicines and no medical use is suggested.

INVOCATIONS

Introduction

Greetings Lightworkers,

We have brought these Invocations through to assist you in this incarnation on planet Earth. There are seven to eight million Lightworkers embodied at this time, to assist in this planet's ascension to the Light dimensions.

These Invocations are designed to support you in building your Light Body, embodying Spirit, healing and balancing your bodies, and walking the Path of Joy.

The Invocations to the Rays have many uses: healing for yourself or others, opening into higher dimensions, accessing information and energies, protection, and transformation. We suggest that you become familiar with these emanations of Light. Also, we advise you to combine the Silver Ray of Grace with any Ray you are visualizing, allowing it to become iridescent and sparkling!

The Invocations of Qualities can be used along with the Rays. They correspond to some aspect of the Emanation. They can also be used alone, when you want to foster a special quality in yourself or your space.

These Invocations are encoded phrases. That means that there are layers of energy placed in each word. Therefore, we advise that you not change the words.

We thank you for your presence on the planet at this time. Your service and dedication to the Light is beautiful to behold.

Ask, and all will be given to assist you. We love you and we are always with you.

Of the Source in Service to the Source,

— Archangel Ariel

INVOCATION TO CLARITY

I stand within the Infinite NOW;
All roads are open to me.
I love within the Infinite NOW;
All paths are clear to me.
I laugh within the Infinite NOW;
All ways are known to me.
Within the Infinite NOW lies all Power.
Within the Infinite NOW lies all Love.
Within the Infinite NOW lies all clarity.
I act within the flow of Spirit,
Acting, loving, knowing
All That Is.

INVOCATION TO UNITY

I AM a Christed Being.
I AM in unity with Spirit.
I AM a Christed Being.
I AM in unity with All That Is.
The Light of my own Being
Shines upon my path.
I AM a Christed Being.
I AM in unity with All That Will Be.
I hold the shining Light of the Source
Within my heart.
I walk in unity with Spirit.
I laugh in unity with the Source.
I love in unity with my fellow beings.
I AM a Christed Being.
I AM a bridge between Heaven and Earth.

INVOCATION TO THE RED RAY

I call upon the Elohim
Of the Ruby Red Ray,
To pour your Light through my body.
I call upon the Elohim
Of the Ruby Red Ray,
To pour the Strength of the Source
Through every cell of my body,
To re-create my body in Light.
May the Ruby Light
Heal all cellular damage,
Release all stress and pain,
Calm all fear of change.
My body is whole in the Light.
My being is calm in the Light.
I have the strength of the Source.

INVOCATION TO TRANQUILITY

I go within
And open the petals of the Crystal Lotus
I go within,
And as the Lotus blooms,
My mind, my body, and emotions quiet.
As my consciousness steps
Into the center of the Lotus,
I become tranquil with who I AM.
I flow with the serenity of Spirit.
As I sit within the Lotus,
I know the Buddha that is Myself.

INVOCATION TO THE ORANGE RAY

I call upon the Elohim
Of the Carnelian Ray,

To pour the Vitality of God
Through my body.
I call upon the Orange Ray,
To awaken my Divine Creativity.
I call upon the Orange Ray,
To deepen my Love and connection
To the planet.
I AM a Master of flow and change,
I feel the beauty of all of Creation.

INVOCATION TO CREATIVITY

I bubble with Divine Expression.
The spark of creativity
Is the spark of Life.
I sculpt realities like fine clay.
I AM the Master artisan of my Life,
I create Visions of the planet in Light
And, behold, the Light is there.
I paint portraits of kind persons
And, behold, more Love is in the world.
I sing of the movement of Spirit
And, behold, I AM soaring.

INVOCATION TO THE YELLOW RAY

I call upon the Elohim
Of the Topaz Ray,
To pour Divine Realization
Through my body.
Through the Yellow Ray
I awaken my Divine Purpose.
I call upon the Yellow Ray,
To strengthen my sense of service
To the Source's Vision.
I call upon the Topaz Ray,

To soften my ego,
That I may surrender to Spirit.

INVOCATION TO AWAKENING

I call the child that I AM
To take my hand and teach me Joy.
I call the child that I AM
To show me the delight of discovery
In all the worlds that I AM.
I take my hand and dance
With the patterns of the Galaxies.
I open my heart and sing
With the patterns of Mastery.
I AM the child that I AM
And I awaken all that I can be.
I awaken I AM.

INVOCATION TO THE GREEN RAY

I call upon the Elohim
Of the Emerald Green Ray,
To pour abundance through my body.
I call upon the Elohim
Of the Emerald Green Ray,
To connect me with my Divine Flow.
As is above, so is below.
I call upon the Green Ray
To strengthen
The opening of my heart, completely.
I call upon the Emerald Ray
To assist my creation of abundance.
As is above, so is below,
All is Love, All is Flow.

INVOCATION TO DIVINE FLOW

I AM the Universe, re-creating myself.
I AM the Universe flowing
To myself, through myself, from myself,
Creating all I see.
I AM the Divine Flow of All That Is.
Abundant is my motion.
I AM the Universe, re-creating myself
To flow abundance.

INVOCATION TO THE BLUE RAY

I call upon the Elohim
Of the Sapphire Blue Ray,
To pour the Light of Sacred Translation
Through my body.

I call upon the Elohim
Of the Sapphire Ray,
To pour Divine Truth
Through my body,
That I may speak the Truth
Of who I AM.

I call upon the Sapphire Blue Ray
To assist me in communicating Love,
And my translation of light to Light.
I call upon the Elohim
Of the Sapphire Blue Ray,
To sweeten my voice so that all
Will hear the Truth of God.

INVOCATION TO LAUGHTER

Some say that laughter is the best medicine.

Some say that laughter is the antidote to sin.
Some say that laughter is a waste of good time.
I tell you laughter is fully Divine.
This planet has a bunch of serious folks,
They just don't get The Cosmic Joke.
And some spend their lives in hot pursuit
Of what they call a Cosmic Truth.
But I heard a joke in the Heavens above ...
Laughter is Truth —
And the punch line is Love.

INVOCATION TO THE INDIGO RAY

I call upon the Elohim
Of the Indigo Ray,
To awaken and strengthen my third and fourth eyes,
For I now choose to See.
I call upon the Elohim of the Star Sapphire Ray,
To awaken the Star
That holds the memories of who I AM.
I call upon the Elohim of the Indigo Ray,
To activate the recorder cell
That I may remember and understand.

INVOCATION TO THE UNIVERSE

I AM the Universe.
I AM the spin and swirl of galaxies.
I AM the movement of planets in their orbits.
I AM a comet in the night sky.
I AM a human being
Moving with the flow of Spirit.
I AM an atom
Containing All That Is.
I AM the Universe,
Laughing as I dance.

I AM Life.

INVOCATION TO THE VIOLET RAY

I call upon the Elohim
Of the Violet Ray,
To pour Divine Transmutation
Through all that I AM.
I call upon the Amethyst Ray
To transform every cell,
Every atom of my bodies
Into Higher Light.
I call upon the Violet Flame
To burn within my soul
And release all veils that separate me
From Spirit.
I call upon the Violet Flame
To burn away my illusions,
To burn away my resistances,
And transmute my fear to Love.

INVOCATION OF THE KEEPERS OF THE FLAME

I AM a Keeper of the Flame.
I carry it forth
Into every part of this world.
I AM a Keeper of the Flame.
I carry it forth
Into every part of my being.
I hold the Flame of God high
So that all may see the shining Light
Of the Divine Plan.
I AM a Keeper of the Flame
And I carry it forth into many worlds,
So that all may know the Light
And carry it onward.

INVOCATION TO THE GOLD RAY

I call upon the Elohim of the Gold Ray
To pour Divine Wisdom into my consciousness.
I call upon the Elohim of the Gold Ray
To reveal the Weights and Measures,
The Balance and Proportions
Of the Universe.
I call upon the Elohim of the Gold Ray
To illuminate my mind,
So it will grow peaceful
With Understanding.
May I be wise in my actions,
Balanced in my emotions,
Peaceful in my mind.

INVOCATION TO MASTERY

I AM a Master,
Dancing through dimensions.
I AM a Master of possibilities,
Weaving the tomorrows into NOW.
I AM a Master of balance,
Skipping on the tightrope of Life.
I AM a Master
Whose strength is compassion.
I AM a Master
Who plays with infinity.
I AM a Master
Who tickles the stars.

INVOCATION TO THE SILVER RAY

I call upon the Elohim of the Silver Ray
To pour Divine Grace through my bodies.

I call upon the Elohim of the Silver Ray
To release all karmic patterns,
To release all pockets of resentment,
That I may know Joy.

I call upon the Elohim of Grace
To fill my being with forgiveness,
To fill my life with gratitude,
And fill my heart with celebration.

I call upon the Elohim of the Silver Ray
To release my bindings of pettiness,
To break the yoke of hatred,
And free my soul.

I call upon the Elohim of Grace
To fill me with the Joy of Living —
NOW.

INVOCATION TO JOY

I have a tickle in my toes
That makes me dance down the street.
I have a giggle in my belly
That makes me hug all I see.
I have a fountain in my heart
That splashes love on the world.
I know the Joy of Spirit
So I laugh in my soul.
I have Joy in living
So I celebrate the Light.

INVOCATION TO THE COPPER RAY

I call upon the Elohim of the Copper Ray
To show me the Divine Blueprint of Life.

I call upon the Elohim of the Copper Ray
To show me the patterns
Of my existence.
I ask that the Copper Ray
Connect and sustain all the primary rays
Through my bodies.
I call upon the Elohim of the Copper Ray
To lead me in the spiral dance,
So that I may ascend to Light.

INVOCATION TO THE SPIRAL DANCE

From my center I call the spiral.
I spin. I glow.
From the center, I grow the spiral
In the home of my soul.
I expand my soul and set it to spin.
In my body, the dance begins.
The spiral grows, its apex in the heart.
It surrounds my body, the vibration starts.
From the Highest Spirit to the soul,
As is above, so is below.
Another spiral, from the Christ,
Created from a Higher Light,
Matches the other with perfect spin
And brings the apex deep within.
Where they touch, a flame, so bright,
Pulls my body into Light.
For it is the Christ within
That puts the galaxies to spin.
In the Light I AM entranced,
Let us lead the spiral dance.

INVOCATION TO THE TURQUOISE RAY

I call upon the Elohim of the Turquoise Ray

To lead me through the Ocean
Of Divine Consciousness.
I call upon the Turquoise Ray
To connect me with all my incarnations.
I call upon the Turquoise Ray
To connect me with all my manifestations.
I AM one with the Greater Consciousness.
I AM Divine Connection,
We dive into the Light and Laugh.

INVOCATION TO FLIGHT

I feel the tingling in my back.
I feel the weight in my shoulders.
I feel the spreading of my wings.
Preparing to fly,
I hear the call of the wind.
I smell the freedom of the skies.
I touch the edge of wonder,
As I begin to lift.
I love the feel of soaring.
I know the thrill of diving.
I light the sky with brilliance,
As I kiss the face of God.

INVOCATION TO THE PINK RAY

I call upon the Elohim of the Pink Ray
To pour forth Divine Unity.
I call upon the Elohim of the Pink Ray
To assist me in accepting
My Christ Self.
I call upon the Elohim of the Pink Ray
To pour Divine Love through my bodies.
May the Love of the Christ
Flow through me.

May the Unity of Spirit
Work through me.
I AM a Christed Being.
I AM in Unity with the Source.

INVOCATION TO SERVICE

I ask in the Name of the Christ,
That I be sustained in the Light.
I ask in the Name of God,
That I be guided and assisted
In my service to the One.
I ask in the Name of the Source,
That the Holy Spirit Shekhina
Fill me with Her Gifts,
That I may serve more fully.
I ask in the Name Yod-Hey-Vav-Hey,
That I may serve the Light
In this world.

INVOCATION TO THE RAY OF RAPTURE

I call upon the Elohim
Of the Ray of Rapture
To pour your Light around my bodies.
I call upon the Ray of Rapture
To assist me in building
My vehicle of Light.
I call upon the Elohim of Rapture
To connect me to the I AM Presence.
I call upon the Elohim of Rapture
To merge me with my Source.

The closest description of the color of this Ray is gold, copper, bronzish honey. Imagine the combined color of all the Rays right before they merge to White. Also, the Ray of Rapture is often experienced as much thicker than the other Rays, much like honey.

INVOCATION TO THE I AM PRESENCE

Ehyah Asher Ehyah.
I AM THAT I AM.
I call upon the Fellowships of Light,
I call upon the Guardians of Light,
I call upon the Angels of Light,
To assist me as I AM
To be who I AM
Linking me to I AM.
Ehyah Asher Ehyah.
I AM THAT I AM.

INVOCATION TO THE WHITE RAY

I call upon the Elohim of the White Ray
To pour the full crystalline
Light of the Source
Through every part of my being.
I call upon the Elohim of the White Ray
To activate the crystal templates
Of my bodies.
I ask that I be attuned
To the fullness of the White Ray,
So that I may be fulfilled.
I call upon the Elohim of the White Ray
To fill me with the Light of God.

INVOCATION TO KIDDUSH HA-SHEM

Blessed is Yod-Hey-Vav-Hey.
Kodosh! Kodosh! Kodosh!
Holy! Holy! Holy!

King of the Universes,
You who set the Divine Order,
May You set the order of my life
According to Your Will.
Blessed is Yod-Hey-Vav-Hey.
Kodosh! Kodosh! Kodosh! Adonai Tsebayot.
Infinite Light.
Infinite Love.
Infinite Truth.
Lord God of Hosts,
May Your Glory cover the Earth.
May your Light sustain the Earth
As It sustains the Heavens.
Holy! Holy! Holy!
Is the Lord God of Hosts.
May the Earth be covered in your Glory.
In this world and the World to Come.
Kodosh! Kodosh! Kodosh!
Adonai Tsebayot.
Maloch Kol Ha-aretz K'vodoh!
Lay-olam Vo-ed.
Amen. Amen. Amen. Amen.

AMEN

I AM a temple of the Light. Amen.
I AM a guardian of the Sacred Arc of the Covenant.
I carry the Laws of God within my heart.
I step between the veils.
I speak with my Source.
Amen.
I AM a temple of the Light. Amen.
I shine forth the letters of the Holy Name from my brow.
I AM a guardian of the Threefold Flame of the Ein Soph.

I AM a priest within the temple of my spirit.
Amen.
I AM a temple of the Light. Amen.
I AM a guardian of the Sacred Arc of the Covenant.
I shine forth the flame of the letters to the world,
So that all may be a temple of the Light,
Keepers of the covenant.
I AM a temple of the Light. Amen.
I AM a guardian of the Sacred Arc of the Covenant.
Amen. Amen. Amen. Amen.

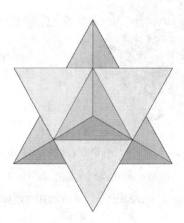

SOURCES

What is Lightbody serves as an introduction to the work of Tashira Tachi-ren. There is much more material to access. Tashira Tachi-ren was on the planet for twelve years. In that time, she generated a tremendous amount of invaluable information, techniques, tools, potions, events, etc. This material, known as the *Angelic Outreach Foundational Work,* is available in the form of audiocassettes, video-tapes, and potions though *Alchemical Mage.*

Since Tashira walked out and Aliyah Ziondra walked in, a whole new level of work has emerged under the name *Wings of Glory.* Aliyah's work stands on its own. However, for those who have worked with the Angelic Outreach material, you will find that *Wings of Glory* dovetails beautifully. To request Aliyah's current catalogue of her individual sessions called the *Shefa Services* book call (503) 321-5111 or send an e-mail to rapture@teleport.com. Check out her website at www.einsoph.com.

All of the works of Tashira Tachi-ren and Aliyah Ziondra, as well as Etherium Technologies and other goodies, are available through Alchemical Mage. To request a catalogue contact:

ALCHEMICAL MAGE
PO Box 31645
Aurora, CO 80041-1645
Phone: (303) 326 - 0924
Fax: (303) 326 - 0928
E-mail: info@alchemicalmage.com

View the Alchemical Mage on-line catalogue at:

www.alchemicalmage.com.

This site also offers a wealth of information, techniques, news, and interactive features. Visit us often!

ORDERFORM

ALCHEMICAL MAGE

P.O. Box 31645
Aurora CO 80041-1645
(303) 326-0924 Phone
(303) 326-0928 FAX
www.alchemicalmage.com
orders@alchemicalmage.com

Name:

Address:

City/State/Zip:

Phone: Day: (   )   Eve: (   )

Method of payment: ☐ Check   or   ☐ Money Order

Payable To: Alchemical Mage

Credit Card: ☐ MasterCard   ☐ Visa

☐ Discover   ☐ American Express

Credit Card Number:

☐☐☐☐☐ ☐☐☐☐☐ ☐☐☐☐☐ ☐☐☐☐☐

Expiration Date: ☐☐ / ☐☐

Name as it appears on Credit Card:

First: M.I.:   Last:

Authorized Signature: Date:

$1 - $30 .... $5.00
$31 - $50 .... $6.00
$51 - $75 .... $7.00
$76 - $100 .... $8.00
$101 - $125 .... $9.00
$126 - $150 .... $10.00
$151 - $175 .... $11.00
$176 - $200 .... $12.00
$201 - $225 .... $13.00
$226 - $250 .... $14.00
$251 - $275 .... $15.00
$276 - $300 .... $16.00

Each Add'l $25.00 Add $1.00

SHIPPING & HANDLING CHART

NOTE: International Orders

For addresses outside of The United States please figure shipping and handling according to the order form then multiply your total p&h by four (4). This figure is your shipping and handling charge. All international orders are shipped UPS Express.

Please pay for all orders in US Dollars ($).
Thank you.

Code	Name	QTY	Price $	Total
01001	ADAM KADMON		15.00	
01002	ALIGNMENT		15.00	
01003	ALPHA OMEGA		15.00	
01004	CO-CREATION		15.00	
01005	DIVINE EXPRESSION		15.00	
01006	DIVINE MOTHER		15.00	
01007	ECSTASY		15.00	
01008	ESSENTIAL EVOLUT. ENCODEMENTS (E-3)		15.00	
01009	EXULTATION		15.00	
01010	FIRE OF PURPOSE		15.00	
01011	GIFTS OF THE HOLY SPIRIT		15.00	
01012	HEAVENLY BODY		15.00	
01013	LOVE POTION # 9		15.00	
01014	MAGICAL VISIONS		15.00	
01015	MAGNIFICENCE		15.00	
01016	MASTERY		15.00	
01017	MERKABAH		15.00	
01018	MYSTICAL ARTICULATION		15.00	
01019	PARADIGM SHIFT		15.00	
01020	PATHCUTTER		15.00	
01021	PLANETARY SERVICE		15.00	
01022	QUANTUM WEALTH		15.00	
01023	SERENITY		15.00	
01024	SERVICE ONE-ON-ONE		15.00	
01025	SUBATOMIC TONIC		15.00	
01026	SURRENDER		15.00	
01027	TRANSCENDENCE		15.00	
01028	TRANSPERSONAL TRANSFORMATION		15.00	
01029	UNIVERSAL DETOX		15.00	
01030	YOD		15.00	
	Potion Sets:			
03001	SET OF ALL ANGELIC OUTREACH POTIONS including Home Sweet Home Enviro-Pack		382.00	
03002	HOME SWEET HOME ENVIRO-PACK		28.00	
03003	SURF'S UP		49.00	
00002	**CATALOG** (including Tools & Techniques)		3.00	
			Sub-Total	
	Sales Taxes 7.55% (CO Residents only)			
		Shipping and Handling		
		GRAND TOTAL: